## welcom━━━━━━━━━━

A new house. A different flat. A shift in the way you live. If you haven't experienced at least one of these developments since 1996, get ready.

Women born between 24 October and 22 November are first in line for a big shift on the home front. By 2003, you may be adjusting to regular U-turns. Just when you thought it was safe to go back to the couch . . . bang. Uranus is your new millennium planet, and it's the planet of change, highlighting anything that's alternative or unexpected in your life. But the end result is a set-up that gives you more freedom, for practical or emotional reasons.

Check your horoscope hot zones (right) for the big picture. You'll see work and health in there too, and your private self – but for more on these, turn the page . . .

*Jessica Adams*
*www.jessicaadams.com.au*

Jessica Adams
# Handbag Horoscopes

# *Scorpio*

## 24 October–22 November

Penguin Books

Penguin Books Australia Ltd
487 Maroondah Highway, PO Box 257
Ringwood, Victoria 3134, Australia
Penguin Books Ltd
Harmondsworth, Middlesex, England
Penguin Putnam Inc.
375 Hudson Street, New York, New York 10014, USA
Penguin Books Canada Limited
10 Alcorn Avenue, Toronto, Ontario, Canada M4V 3B2
Penguin Books (NZ) Ltd
Cnr Rosedale and Airborne Roads, Albany, Auckland, New Zealand
Penguin Books (South Africa) (Pty) Ltd
5 Watkins Street, Denver Ext 4, 2094, South Africa
Penguin Books India (P) Ltd
11, Community Centre, Panchsheel Park, New Delhi 110 017, India

First published by Penguin Books Australia Ltd 1999

10 9 8 7 6 5 4 3 2

Copyright © Jessica Adams, 1999

Cover design by Yolande Gray
Props by Sacha Dunn
Text design by Debra Billson, Penguin Design Studio
Typeset in Gill Sans and Bodoni by Midland Typesetters, Maryborough, Victoria
Printed in Australia by Australian Print Group, Maryborough, Victoria

National Library of Australia
Cataloguing-in-Publication data:

Adams, Jessica.
  Scorpio.

  ISBN 0 14 028620 9.

  1. Scorpio (Astrology). 2. Horoscopes. I. Title. (Series: Handbag horoscopes).

133.5273

www.penguin.com.au

# *acknowledgements*

When I was seven years old, I read a book called *Catweazle and the Magic Zodiac*, by Richard Carpenter. Catweazle was a magician, and he was looking for the twelve star signs. In fact, he spent his entire time rushing around the English countryside on a tricycle, hunting them down.

As I was writing each Handbag Horoscope, I was reminded of Catweazle. And I would like to thank him for converting me to astrology at the age of seven. It was much more interesting than Barbie dolls, and it still is.

Handbag Horoscopes began as a scribbled idea on a note-pad. Alison Cowan, Julie Gibbs and Gaby Naher turned the idea into something real. Thank you! I would also like to thank Electric Ephemeris and Adam Smith for their help with the tables.

*Part proceeds from the sale of Handbag Horoscopes will be donated to War Child, a charity which benefits child survivors of war. The War Child web site address is www.warchild.com.*

# contents

# one

## astrology works – and here's the proof

Here are the big five arguments against astrology. You've probably heard them all before:

1  *Newspaper and magazine predictions are too general – they could mean anything.*
2  *How can the planets affect our lives when they're so far away?*
3  *Astrologers just make it up.*
4  *How can the future be the same for one in twelve people?*
5  *If astrology works, why aren't all astrologers millionaires?*

**OK, get ready for the five big answers:**

I write horoscope prediction columns for many magazines around the world, including *Cosmopolitan* and *New Woman*. They are general predictions because media astrology is a general business. I only know your Star Sign, after all – I don't know your Rising Sign, or your Moon Sign, or anything about your midheaven – and these really matter.

However, some things really stand out. Because you're a Scorpio, I know that independence and freedom have been recurring issues in your family since 1996. That is a general statement, based on the fact that Uranus, the planet of freedom, has recently been in the 4th House, which is your department of family relationships.

I can't nail it down to specifics about your family life in my columns because I don't know if you are close to your parents, an orphan, not on speaking terms with your father or still living with your grandmother at the age of 45. Neither does any astrologer. That's why we can only predict your future in fairly general terms, talking about a broad concept like freedom in family relationships.

It's a bit like weather forecasters. They can only ever tell you about possible showers over certain parts of your area.

Because they have to take in such a large audience living all over the place, they have to make sweeping generalisations. They could probably tell you that at five minutes past one when you open your front door it's going to pour down with rain, but only if you get the forecaster over for a personal consultation!

It's the same with astrology. A personal horoscope consultation (based on the time, date and year of your birth) will be stunningly accurate, specific and detailed in the hands of a good astrologer. In the meantime, magazine and newspaper forecasts are pretty damn good. Not all the time. But most of the time. Want to hear some?

**The Experiment Subject: Hillary Clinton (Scorpio)**
**The Event: Bill Clinton's affair with Monica**
**Lewinsky goes public**
**The Date: August 1998**

✵ **The Astrologer:** Elizabeth Potier
   **The Magazine:** US *Elle*
   **She Said:** Scorpio – 'Around the 21st, ask yourself
   "Are others being dishonest or simply stupid?"
   Perhaps a little of both. Find your forgiveness zone

and remember that sometimes happiness depends
on how much you can overlook.'

✸ **The Astrologer:** Marjorie Orr
  **The Magazine:** UK *Saturday*
  **She Said:** Scorpio – 'There may be muddles and
  misunderstandings with family members which
  make you panic on and off until August when you
  need to be firm but fair. Lay your cards on the
  table and insist everyone else does the same. June
  to September could be a cooling period with certain
  close mates. Saturn is pointing out flaws and
  inadequacies. In certain relationships this could
  mean a parting of the ways.'

One of the things that makes a great astrology column is
the smart advice, as well as the accuracy of the prediction.
And that's basically what it's all about. By looking at the
positions of the planets in the heavens, astrologers who
know their stuff can give you time-honoured advice, based
on at least 500 years of testing and research by the stargazers who have gone before. They can give you insights
so that you are free to make a more informed choice about
your life. We call it predicting, but of course, it's only the

fact that a column is printed at the beginning of the month that turns the words into predictions. Astrology's real function is to explain the present. To look at it in terms of opportunities not to be missed and painful experiences to be understood, or even avoided.

Even though you might accept astrology works, though, how do you get your head around the fact that a distant planet like Pluto can possibly affect a woman down here on planet earth?

There are many explanations of the 'how it works' variety. Read *The Scientific Basis Of Astrology*, by Percy Seymour, if you need to know more. Basically, what I do is just pick up a hefty book and chuck it at sceptics. They're quite heavy in hardback and make good ammunition. A sceptic, by the way, is usually someone who read the side of a Snoopy Star Sign coffee mug in 1973 and has based their entire argument on that.

Excuse me for getting a little obstreperous here. But after all, I do this for a living. And no, I don't make it up (neither does any other media astrologer, to the best of my knowledge).

I know it might sound strange that just because you are a Scorpio, you can be going through the same basic life experiences as one-twelfth of the population. Think of Star Signs as being similar to gender, though, and it doesn't look quite so weird. Women have repeated life patterns: we have the menstrual cycle to deal with, just because we were born female; we also know in advance when we're likely to experience the menopause; and when we get pregnant we can usually predict the timed outcome of that too! Being born under the label 'woman' means you'll go through life with a higher-pitched voice, among other things. At the end of the day, astrological labelling isn't that different. It's all cosmic number crunching, and knowing you're a Scorpio or an Aquarius, or whatever, is no more mysterious than knowing you're a woman. Based on what astrologers know about these signs, they can also make predictions for you, or talk about general characteristics.

And, by the way, there is no such thing as a cusp. You really are either one sign or the other. Give your birth details to an astrologer and they can sort it all out for you.

This knowledge is enough to make astrologers – or their clients – wealthy. And quite a few of them are (though they don't talk about it much). However, in order to make millions from this business, you have to be born with the sort of birth horoscope that leans towards you being good with money or lucky with deals. If you were born with a tricky cash chart, you can time Jupiter trines to the 2nd House for all you are worth (sorry, I had to stick some astro-lingo in there!) and you're still not going to take Ivana Trump out to lunch.

Astrology works. It's so accurate that sometimes I believe what it tells me even when the evidence is going against it. In December 1996, *New Weekly* magazine in Australia asked me to predict Brad Pitt's year ahead. They were carrying stories about his blissful romance with Gwyneth Paltrow at the time, and photographs of them in pool-side full-frontal hugs. It wasn't easy to print this, but after looking at Brad's chart, I had to do it.

*New Weekly*, **December 1996**: 'Brad's relationship with Gwyneth Paltrow has been formed at a time when he is not 100 per cent clear about what he wants or needs. It will be tested out in 1997, when one of them will have to deal with a cooling-off period.'

In June 1997 they split up.

I wrote Emma Thompson's year-ahead prediction on her birthday.

*New Weekly*, April 1995: 'Emma's love life this year looks very complicated. She faces some difficult questions with husband Kenneth Branagh in April and June.'

Six months later, they separated.

Good astrologers never, ever predict actual separation or divorce – firstly on the grounds that they wouldn't want to hear it, so why would you? And secondly on the grounds that it's impossible. Clairvoyants predict specific events. Astrologers can only predict general moods and trends. If you choose to do something major, like leave your husband, that's your business. We can only tell you the emotional weather at the time and hopefully guide your decision by supplying extra information and insight.

Finally, let's be real about this. It doesn't work with 100 per cent accuracy all the time. This may be because astrologers are only human and, like doctors, they occasionally make a wrong diagnosis. It may also be because of the planet Uranus, which rules chaos theory, and consequently mucks everything up now and again – and Neptune, which rules confusion. Astrologers accept that Uranus and Neptune are part of the deal, and if we do that, we also have to live with the fact that our insights will sometimes be wrong, because that's what these planets stand for – chaos and confusion! The occasional wrong call may even be part of the greater pattern that makes most of it right.

For the most part, though, astrology will work for you if you let it, and it's like weather forecasting for the soul. Did you know that most magazine astrologers have to send in their columns over three months before the issue appears in the newsagents? In year-ahead predictions we are often working a whole 12 months into the future. Sceptics and some prejudiced scientists knock us, but we are prepared to go into print, and on the record, ahead of time – every time.

Here's Penny Thornton (former astrologer to Princess

Diana) predicting Bill Clinton's year ahead in January 1998, in Australia's *Who Weekly* magazine: 'He seems invulnerable to anything the cosmos can throw at him and will ride through 1998's holocausts. The scandals won't stop, but if he's emerged smelling like a rose before, he'll do it again.'

My advice is to check astrology, test it and use it. It's there so you can understand what the hell is actually going on when things are bad, and so that you can energetically exploit life's more fabulous opportunities when they come your way.

# two

## what it *really* means
## to be a scorpio woman

Okay. Let's start at the beginning and be straight about this. Here's what you're not –

**Vindictive. Stubborn. Unforgiving.**

A lot of rubbish gets written about your sign. This is because someone made it all up in about 1930 and it's just been recycled ever since. I've seen the most bizarre things about Scorpio printed inside birthday cards ('You have sexual stamina'). Well, that's nice for your ego, but it has nothing to do with astrology – or what it really means to be a Scorpio.

How does a sign get 'given' characteristics anyway? It

began with the first stargazers, who noticed that people born when the sun appeared to be passing through a certain zodiac constellation seemed to have traits in common. The pattern of stars that makes up Scorpio could really be anything – a bank teller, a map of Africa, a hamburger. The fact that the ancients decided the stars joined together to make the shape of a scorpion is significant, though.

Scorpions are survivors. We know this because their sting is either painful or (in a few cases) deadly, making them excellent attackers and defenders. They also survive radiation: when the French ran nuclear weapons tests in the Sahara Desert, scorpions survived. Ancient astrologers discovered that people born in late October or early November have similar survival skills. In times of crisis, you have the ability to survive psychologically. If you are sacked, made redundant or reduced to bankruptcy, you will crawl out of your hiding place after the bomb has gone off in your life, surprisingly intact, and scramble back on track. Your spirit never dies, and that's the truth.

Here's something else about Scorpio – complex sexuality. That doesn't mean you're a sex maniac, waving your tasselled bra in the air. It just means sex for you is deep, intense, complicated and multi-faceted. Scorpions will mate, then kill each other. In some species, the male stings the female to sedate her, then pulls her towards him to have sex. Human sex can be just as complex. But you understand it.

## scorpio realities

🔒 *You survive crisis – psychologically, spiritually, emotionally and physically.*

🔒 *You instinctively know what an intense business sex can be, for better or worse.*

🔒 *Even if you never actually hurt or destroy anyone, the fact that other people know you are capable of doing this is enough to give you a great deal of power.*

**'I have a little bit of penis envy. They're ridiculous, but they're cool.'**
**k.d. lang, born 2 November 1961**

### *the strongest sign?*

In interviews with Scorpios, something interesting emerges: you agree with statements such as 'I enjoy convincing others' and 'I can get my way and assert myself', but tend to disagree with statements along the lines of 'I think I'm going to be successful'.

Maybe this is because you *know* you're going to be successful – or because you already are! But this research (outlined in *The Astrology File*, written by Gunter Sachs) seems to support the idea that Scorpio is one of the strongest signs in the zodiac.

## who do you get on with?

It's wrong to say that you're most compatible with Pisces or Cancer – or that you don't get on with Taurus. You've probably read things like that everywhere, but in actual fact you need to have full horoscopes drawn up for you and your partner if you want to know the whole truth. A relationship or a marriage is extremely complicated, and so is astrology. That's why comparing something as basic as Star Signs gets you nowhere!

For the real story you need to see a professional astrologer:

🔖 *Your Moon Sign will have to be compared to your man's chart to see how you'll feel about living together or starting a family. How would you deal with illness, miscarriage or moving house? Your Moon Signs describe if you're going to see life the same way and be there for each other emotionally and domestically.*

🛍 *Your Venus Sign will have to be compared to your man's chart to see how romantic, erotic and loving your relationship's really going to be. If you want a long-term relationship or marriage where the passion never really fades, then you will need strong chemistry based on your Venus Signs.*

🛍 *Your Mercury Sign will have to be compared to his chart, too, to see if there will be communication problems. Will phone calls be easy for both of you, or will it never feel quite right? What about clear understanding and good listening skills? Mercury Signs matter.*

🛍 *Your Mars Sign will have to be compared to his chart to see how both of you are going to handle irritation, anger or stress as a couple. Mars also has an influence on sexual tension, and sex in general. Will you drive each other mad, or can you deal with anger constructively?*

What you can say about chemistry and compatibility is this. What you're actually looking for, in terms of recognising something in a man which is also part of you, lies in chapter six (*profile of your soulmate*). You know that 'click' feeling you get with certain lovers? Part of it comes from identifying certain bits of a bloke's heart, soul or brain that strongly resonate with bits of you. Is your soulmate a star, a thinker, a rock or a caretaker? Skip to page 75 right away to find out. But if you're really serious about long-term chemistry and compatibility, get both your charts compared. The Internet has several sites where you can order these, and other kinds of charts. I recommend The Astrology Shop online at www.astrology.co.uk (it has special sections for the UK, USA and Australia) as a good starting point.

# three

## surfing the stars – how to make the most of the 21st century

In this section, you'll see where the major breakthroughs and plus factors are over the next seven years. If you sit back and do nothing, it's possible that you'll get what you want without trying. However, if you are looking for something major, be proactive. Don't just let fate take you for a ride – double your luck by catching the wave and then getting everything you can from it while it's there. In other words, if your work zone is going off during April 2000, then that's the time to consciously follow up every opportunity. Especially if it involves becoming the boss of Cadbury's and getting free Flakes.

I could give you all sorts of predictions for the 21st

century – job traumas, money hassles, love-life dramas or health problems. After ten years as an astrologer, though, I have come to believe that the most useful thing you can hear is the good stuff. (By the way, I just made all that bad stuff up.) What's on offer to you in this new century? Where's the good news coming from? That's what astrology is all about. Consequently I'm not going to utter any dire warnings or doom and gloom predictions. What I want to do in this section is show you how good life could be – and where the growth spurts are going to come from. The rest is up to you.

## DATELINE: MARCH AND APRIL 2000, 2001, 2003, 2006, 2007
### catch the wave: work, lifestyle, health, wellbeing

The smallest effort to focus on your confidence levels regarding work, daily life or health could see fantastic results in March and April 2000, 2001, 2003, 2006 and 2007. The spotlight will be on your mind–body connection at this time. At the same time, your job, your studies or your household routine will also be in focus. With a little help from Uranus, Neptune and Pluto, you will find that the March–April period of these years brings excitement and pride in yourself, inspiration and confidence, power and glory.

You can lead the way in these months. What develops around you will put you in the right place at the right time to take a starring role in your own working life, studies, daily lifestyle or health. By the way, these will be interconnected issues. So it may be useful to take a closer look at your day and how it measures up in terms of work hours, exercise, eating patterns, relaxation, sleeping, obligations to other people, and chores. Are you expressing yourself in all this? Do you feel confident about the fact that you are truly being yourself? This cycle could put you on track if you need to do that, or just bring life up a few levels.

These months are about finding a sense of ego, pride and strong self-esteem in connection with the basic, daily things that you do as part of your job description, home duties or study schedule. You didn't think something so boring and ordinary could make you feel good about yourself? Wait and see what the planets have in store for you. Astrologically, March–April of these years is a great time to contact authority figures in the life areas described above. Draw a little closer to well-known, respected leaders in their profession or calling – especially if these people impact on your health, fitness, job, study or lifestyle. You won't have to look too far for them: these people stand out anyway, and they will be moving more obviously in your world.

**Five fantasies for March–April 2000, 2001, 2003, 2006, 2007**

1 You win a year's sessions with a personal trainer. You inspire her to invent a new exercise, and she names it after you.

2 Your boss is so impressed by your star performance on a routine job that you're allocated the coveted corner office with a view.

3 A famous health guru hypnotises you. When you wake up, you truly understand the connection between mind, body and spirit for the first time.

4 You hand in an everyday assignment and win a gold-plated student diary.

5 You lead a campaign at work to bring masseurs into the office at lunchtime. Soon, you have your own corporate massage empire.

*Now, make up your own fantasies . . .*

You may be asked to act as an authority figure yourself. Work is an obvious example of where it might happen, but you could also be a leading light in terms of health, wellbeing, lifestyle or fitness for another person. Being proud of yourself for the respect you are getting helps strengthen your sense of identity, not to mention boosting your ego. You shine, and this in turn helps other people to shine. A bit of glory never hurt any woman, and that is exactly what will be on offer during these March–April cycles over the next few years.

Part of the trend is that every detail of your daily life becomes more important. It becomes more obvious. What you eat for breakfast may take on startling significance. How long you take for lunch, and whether you walk to work or spend half an hour gardening at the end of the day. Who does your teeth? What about alternative therapies? Your Filofax, diary or schedule will matter more. You may begin to get the message that efficiency is important, that routines and rituals are crucial.

The work ethic is something you can take pride in now. It has nothing to do with big career coups or dashes to the top. It's really about the small things. How you deal with clients, employers, employees, colleagues or fellow students. If you're at home, how you handle relationships with people there will matter more. You have a clear choice in these March–April cycles. You can be respected, admired, recognised and even worshipped (just a little bit), just so long as you can see why the work ethic matters and how you can turn in a star performance by sticking to it.

You can do your duty to other people, and also to yourself. This particularly applies in terms of your body. Whatever state your health is in (and health really extends beyond the body to the spirit), the March–April planet cycles will help you to take pride in all the rituals and routines that go with your particular body. It may become a source of satisfaction for you that you can improve your heart rate, lower your cholesterol, or walk five steps when you could only walk one the day before. It all depends on your personal situation, naturally, but focus on pride in your own wellbeing.

The mantra for these months is 'Express yourself' and it will be the smallest things, like a swim in the pool, or an afternoon meeting at work, that will put you back in touch with who you are, and how you live it out. On a big scale, one of the years listed on the March–April checklist could see you achieving a major work breakthrough, or hitting a fitness landmark. You could get a new job that allows you to be creative, or to be the boss. You could triumph on a weight-loss regime that is also a psychological transformation for you.

Begin with the basic ideas about working, living, eating, exercising and relaxing and go from there. You might find it interesting to set annual goals that begin on 1 March and end on 30 April.

**In a few words:** Your pride and ego will be linked to work, study, health or wellbeing.
**Look for:** VIP work or study contacts, health and fitness leaders, mind–body gurus.
**If you do nothing:** You'll still get a few moments of glory in your life.
**If you push things:** You could begin a glorious new workstyle or lifestyle.

### DATELINE: SEPTEMBER AND OCTOBER 2000, 2002, 2005, 2006, 2007

## catch the wave: your private self, your life behind the scenes

You have a lot to gain from your private side in these months. Navel-gazing will become more important. You might be analysing your dreams, meditating, keeping a journal, or seeing a therapist. You might be holidaying by yourself, taking a week off work, or taking up a hobby or interest such as bushwalking or yoga which allows you to quietly take stock. By retreating from the noise and madness outside your front door, you will win back something extremely important – yourself. As an astrological prediction, that might not sound very exciting. You may be looking for love, money or success – in no particular order. But the amazing thing about these September–October cycles is that the contact you have with your private self will actually increase and enhance these other areas of your life. Maybe now, maybe later. But getting to know yourself better in private could have fantastic end results.

Secrets have a lot to do with this cycle. Everyone has them. But yours will be more crucial to your confidence in yourself and your life. You may find yourself hiding your light behind a locked door, as you confidently lead the way on a project or special plan that is hush-hush. You're shining, but nobody can see you. Alternatively you may become involved in interests or important challenges that involve you spending more time by yourself, locked away from the world. You could become a classic back-room girl on a creative, attention-grabbing project. Nobody can see what you're doing, but your sense of pride and self-esteem could take off as a result of this solitary mission.

These September–October cycles are very much about

finding yourself. Yes, I know it's a loathsome phrase, but it's surprising how many times women go through the motions of their lives – work, relationships, homes, money, holidays – without being entirely clear about who they are, or why they're doing everything. You may find yourself on the side-lines in these months, like the reserve on a netball team waiting for a game. Fate may ask you to step out for a while, to beat a retreat or to hibernate. You may begin a new job that takes you to a very solitary or locked-up place, behind the scenes somewhere. That's just one possibility. A more mundane one is that you're forced to take time out to recover from a cold. Lying flat on your back in a quiet room, you finally get the insight into yourself you've needed for some time. The importance of building up your ego, pride, vitality, confidence and sense of self in a place that leaves you to your own devices is part of the story.

## Five fantasies for September–October 2000, 2002, 2005, 2006, 2007

1 You become a secret agent and win a military medal under a false name.
2 You go to a health farm and lose five kilos – and all of your insecurity.

3 Secret diaries you've kept for years become bestsellers.
4 Dream researchers name you Dreamer of the Year in 25 countries.
5 You get a job in a psychiatric hospital and realise you're sane – at last.

*Now, make up your own fantasies . . .*

Get used to the idea of being a star behind the scenes. As you go towards 2007, it will become quite a familiar feeling. Your ability to express yourself, to be creative or to take a leading role in a project which means hanging back will be on the agenda. The situation may change, the details and faces may be different each time, but the theme is the same. Glory behind a screen! It's rather like being the scriptwriter for a big Hollywood blockbuster starring Tom Cruise and Nicole Kidman – they get the Oscars, and you're hidden in the credits. Or think of an understudy hanging around back-stage. In your own way, you're getting a (quiet) piece of the glory. This will be a common theme as you go towards October.

The 12th House of the horoscope, which is what this cycle affects, is connected with Pisces and Neptune. That's a pretty watery message. These few weeks will have a fluid, dreamy, imaginative quality about them. A little like scuba diving. A little like lucid dreaming. Imagine a float tank full of blue bath fizz – you're in it.

Private and quiet places lend themselves to this September–October cycle. But the quietest place is probably inside your own head. Your pride, your confidence, your vitality and your radiance will be locked inside something secret, private or solitary at this time. Although this isn't the big showy stuff we're looking at here, these cycles will still be among the most important this millennium for you.

**In a few words:** You don't have to chant 'Om' to find yourself, but you can if you wish.

**Look for:** Dream books, therapists, secret projects, health farms, self-help manuals, meditation teachers, astrologers, psychics, locked filing cabinets.

**If you do nothing:** Your secrets will still be the brightest thing in your life.

**If you push things:** You could star in a behind-the-scenes project.

# four

## dates for your diary

Jupiter, Saturn, Uranus, Neptune and Pluto are the power points of astrology. Between the dates below, you will plug into these power points as the planets make major patterns in your horoscope. A significant event may occur on just one day in the ten-day time spans below. Or you may find something gathers speed over the course of a week or more. You don't have to take Jupiter's opportunities or open yourself up to Uranus's radical changes. But if you feel something going on at these times and you can't quite get it straight in your head, this section may spell it out and help you to focus. These are really important power points in your year, so watch out for them.

Some power points repeat every year. The situation may be different each time, but the issues underneath will be exactly the same. This is why I've left space for your own notes underneath some sections. When you encounter the same Pluto power point, for example, go back to your notes from previous years. This is probably the best thing you can do for yourself in handling the future! By learning from other power point times in the past, you will know a little of what to expect, and you will also know what you did right or wrong last time.

# 2000
## *20–30 january*
## **neptune power point**
**The Focus:** The people who make up your family – close or distant.

**The Issues:** Sacrifice. Intuition. Spirituality. Where do you end and others begin?

**Your Choice:** Kindness can turn you into the star of this particular situation.

**Notes:** This power point will repeat every year until 2005. Take notes on the following page:

---

---

---

---

## 1–11 february
## uranus power point

**The Focus:** The home front – this is a continuing
theme during January and February.

**The Issues:** Honesty. Differences and individuality.
Dealing with change. Space.

**Your Choice:** Be dignified. Be yourself. Create
freedom for yourself or the other person.

**Notes:** This power point will repeat every year until
2003. Take notes here:

---

---

## *4–14 may*
## *jupiter power point*

**The Focus:** Your partners – past, present or future.

**The Issues:** Opportunities. Recognition. Confidence. Total optimism.

**Your Choice:** You can shine now, and take the smallest opportunity and open it up.

**Remember:** This power point will not happen again for 12 years.

## *6–16 may*
## *saturn power point*

**The Focus:** The focus is still on one-on-one situations that push your buttons.

**The Issues:** Patience. Believing in yourself. Taking a reality check. Dealing with heavy stuff.

**Your Choice:** Express yourself, lead the way, or take the spotlight – and take the burden.

**Remember:** This power point will not happen again for 29 years.

## 29 november–9 december
## pluto power point

**The Focus:** Money-related issues. And, on a deeper level, your set of values.

**The Issues:** Transformation. Power. Control.

**Your Choice:** You are who you are, so express it through your values, cash, home or possessions. Change things or find your own power.

**Notes:** This power point will repeat every year until 2005. Take notes here:

-------------------------------------------------------------

-------------------------------------------------------------

-------------------------------------------------------------

# 2001
## 21–31 january
## neptune power point

**The Focus:** It may be your family this time, or it may be the place where you live.

**The Issue:** Floating onto another level to look at what is real – and unreal – about it all.

**Your Choice:** Healthy self-esteem makes it possible to put your ego second.

**Notes:** This power point will repeat every year until 2005. Take notes here:

---

---

## 4–14 february
## uranus power point

**The Focus:** The way you live and the people you live with – or grew up with.

**The Issue:** Allowing lightning bolts to jolt you awake and show you what's true for you.

**Your Choice:** Why stick to old rules, attitudes or set-ups if they no longer work for now?

**Notes:** This power point will repeat every year until 2003. Take notes here:

---

---

## 20–30 may
### saturn power point

**The Focus:** Joint finances. Agreements over money, possessions or property.

**The Issues:** Understanding what responsibility is. Learning from life and other people.

**Your Choice:** Wisdom and experience aren't boring, they're assets to be proud of.

**Notes:** This power point will repeat next year – it's an ongoing theme. Take notes here:

---

---

---

---

---

## 9–19 june
### jupiter power point

**The Focus:** Other people's involvement in your lifestyle or security.

**The Issues:** Luck – is it fate, or do you make it happen? Positive thinking. Opportunities.
**Your Choice:** Confidence and positive thinking go together.
**Remember:** This power point will not happen again for 12 years.

## 2–12 december
### pluto power point

**The Focus:** Your attitude towards what you earn or owe, and what's valuable.
**The Issues:** Going more deeply into things; realising that change is an intense business.
**Your Choice:** Confidence means never being content to live life on the surface.
**Notes:** This power point will repeat every year until 2005. Take notes here:

-----------------------------------------------------------

-----------------------------------------------------------

-----------------------------------------------------------

-----------------------------------------------------------

# 2002
## *20 january–2 february*
## *neptune power point*

**The Focus:** The people or places that give you a sense of belonging.

**The Issue:** Feeling for others as you would feel for yourself, no matter what the situation.

**Your Choice:** Enlightened beings only get that way through kindness.

**Notes:** This power point will repeat every year until 2005. Take notes here:

_____

_____

## *8–18 february*
## *uranus power point*

**The Focus:** Your flat, your house, your family, your household, your roots or origins.

**The Issues:** Life (and people) can be unpredictable, and a wake-up and a shake-up amount to the same thing.

**Your Choice:** True freedom and a greater sense of being alive come with tolerance.
**Notes:** This power point will repeat next year.
Take notes here:

-------------------------------------------------------

-------------------------------------------------------

*4–14 june*
*saturn power point*
**The Focus:** Verbal or paper agreements tying up cash, property or possessions.
**The Issues:** Taking things on board with people. Being a realist. Finding patience.
**Your Choice:** There's something noble about doing all the right things this month.
**Remember:** This power point happened last year, so check your notes on page 34.

*15–25 july*
*jupiter power point*
**The Focus:** Overseas or distant places and faces, wide horizons, big subjects.

The Issues: Seeing the positive; pursuing the possibilities, not the impossibilities.

Your Choice: You can take something small and do a whole lot more with it.

Remember: This power point will not happen again for 12 years.

## 4–14 december
### pluto power point

The Focus: The financial and practical side of life, from shopping to business.

The Issue: Where is your power base or sense of control in any of these areas?

Your Choice: You, or a set-up around you, can be the grub that turns into a butterfly.

Notes: This power point will repeat every year until 2005. Take notes here:

-------------------------------------------------------------

-------------------------------------------------------------

-------------------------------------------------------------

-------------------------------------------------------------

# 2003
## *25 january–4 february*
## *neptune power point*

**The Focus:** Where you fit in, domestically – at home or with your family.

**The Issue:** Knowing that it's sometimes in your own interest to put yourself second.

**Your Choice:** Spiritual, religious, psychic or cosmic people could show you a lot now.

**Notes:** This power point will repeat every year until 2005. Take notes here:

-------------------------------------------------------------------

-------------------------------------------------------------------

## *12–22 february*
## *uranus power point*

**The Focus:** The environments or people that mean home to you.

**The Issue:** Living life in an honest, exciting, completely free way, despite the uncertainty.

**Your Choice:** Your confidence and sense of self fuse with your ability to accept change.

**Remember:** After three years of this cycle, you can now say goodbye to it – what did you learn?

## 17–27 august
## jupiter power point

**The Focus:** Your success rating and status. Your ambitions and goals.

**The Issue:** Looking for the possibilities, the 'yes' answers, the green lights and the luck.

**Your Choice:** Express yourself. Light your own way. Confidence breeds confidence.

**Remember:** This power point will not happen again for 12 years.

## 6–16 december
## pluto power point

**The Focus:** Your cash flow and what you spend it on. Whatever's valuable to you now.

**The Issue:** The one thing you can't talk about, or even face, is the biggest factor now.

**Your Choice:** By examining a taboo or off-limits topic, you open the way to change.

**Notes:** This power point will repeat every year until 2005. Take notes here:

---

---

---

---

*(there is no saturn power point this year)*

## 2004
### *28 january–7 february*
### *neptune power point*
**The Focus:** Flatmates, people at home, close family members or relatives.
**The Issue:** What is the difference between a meaningful sacrifice and martyring yourself?
**Your Choice:** Put yourself in the other person's shoes – whatever their taste in footwear.
**Notes:** This power point will repeat next year. Take notes on the following page:

---

---

---

### 16–26 february
### uranus power point

**The Focus:** Kids, self-expression or romance.

**The Issues:** Being open to a whole new order. Understanding how a lightning bolt can lead to the changes that set you free.

**Your Choice:** Do things differently, break some of your own rules and achieve a breakthrough.

**Notes:** This power point will repeat next year. Take notes here:

---

---

---

## *3–13 july*
## *saturn power point*

**The Focus:** People or locations out of town or off the map. Study or big ideas.

**The Issues:** Accepting life as it is, not as you would like it to be. Hanging in there.

**Your Choice:** There's a kind of glory in being open to basic learning experiences.

**Remember:** This power point will not happen again for 29 years.

## *17–27 september*
## *jupiter power point*

**The Focus:** Friendships, old and new. Groups of people around you.

**The Issue:** Your sense of self (and identity) will be bound up with these people.

**Your Choice:** Whatever is important to you could grow, but it all begins with total optimism.

**Remember:** This power point will not happen again for 12 years.

## 9–19 december
## pluto power point

**The Focus:** Small stuff (shopping) and big stuff (income). What's it worth?

**The Issues:** Dealing with intensity in yourself or others. And the balance of power between people.

**Your Choice:** Before you change a set-up, you have to change yourself.

**Notes:** This power point will repeat every year until 2005. Take notes here:

-----------------------------------------------------------------

-----------------------------------------------------------------

## 2005
## 30 january–9 february
## neptune power point

**The Focus:** Layer upon layer inside yourself that tells the full story about a parent.

**The Issue:** Blurring the boundaries means you see what Buddha saw – that we are all one – and that includes family.

**Your Choice:** Feeling proud of yourself begins with

your choice to sympathise or empathise with others.
**Remember:** Your notes from Neptune power points
in previous years could be useful now.

## *20 february–2 march*
## *uranus power point*
**The Focus:** A brainchild, or a real child in your life.
The third option? Love.
**The Issues:** Radical change. Independence in yourself
or another. Being true to yourself. Respecting yourself
and others for doing or saying what is honest.
**Your Choice:** You know who you are, and love, kids
or creativity reveals it.
**Remember:** Your notes from 2004 could be useful now.

## *19–29 july*
## *saturn power point*
**The Focus:** Your direction in life. Where you're
heading, professionally or socially.
**The Issues:** Accepting what you cannot change.
Developing patience.
**Your Choice:** If something about yourself is a serious
matter, then take it seriously.

**Remember:** This power point will happen again next year!

## *16–26 october*
## *jupiter power point*
**The Focus:** The hidden part of yourself.
**The Issue:** If you think you can make it happen, then you probably *can* make it happen.
**Your Choice:** Recognise a lucky break when you see it, no matter what form it takes.
**Remember:** Read 'catch the wave: your private self, your life behind the scenes', on page 23, too.

## *11–21 december*
## *pluto power point*
**The Focus:** What being rich actually means. By now you know the answer!
**The Issue:** A natural cycle is unfolding – like a plant growing, dying and producing seeds.
**Your Choice:** Resurrect something. Or get rid of one thing so another can grow.
**Remember:** Your notes from previous years could be useful now.

# five

### your venus sign –
### is this the real you?

Not knowing your Venus Sign is like not knowing that
you're a Scorpio. It's just as important. Most of the time,
it's actually different from your Star Sign – you might be a
Scorpio with a Sagittarius Venus Sign or a Libra Venus Sign.
Women often tell me that they feel their Venus Sign is really
'them'. Their Star Sign is in there too, but it's the Venus
Sign which is really accurate.

It's not surprising, really. Venus is a female planet. When
you fall in love, buy clothes, put on perfume or hang out
with your girlfriends, you tend to live out the personality
qualities of your Venus Sign. If you go to parties and people
try to guess if you're an Aries or a Taurus or whatever

(how annoying!) they might get your Venus Sign, not your Star Sign.

To find out your Venus Sign, look up your day and year of birth in the tables on the following pages. These show the change-over dates, so start with the month on the left-hand side and then work across to find which sign Venus was in when you were born. For example, if you were born on 5 January 1960, your Venus Sign is Sagittarius, but if you were born on 28 January of that year, then your Venus Sign is Capricorn.

If your birthday falls outside the years shown in these tables, check out www.astro.com on the Internet – it'll give you a free run-down of all your planets.

Don't worry if your Venus Sign is the same as your Star Sign – in other words, you happen to have a Scorpio Venus Sign too. It just makes you a classic double Scorpio! In most cases, though, you're about to discover a whole new side of yourself . . .

**1949**

| MTH | DAY | SIGN |
| --- | --- | --- |
| JAN | 1 | SAG |
| JAN | 13 | CAP |
| FEB | 6 | AQU |
| MAR | 2 | PIS |
| MAR | 26 | ARI |
| APR | 19 | TAU |
| MAY | 14 | GEM |
| JUN | 7 | CAN |
| JUL | 1 | LEO |
| JUL | 26 | VIR |
| AUG | 20 | LIB |
| SEP | 14 | SCO |
| OCT | 10 | SAG |
| NOV | 6 | CAP |
| DEC | 6 | AQU |

**1950**

| MTH | DAY | SIGN |
| --- | --- | --- |
| JAN | 1 | AQU |
| APR | 6 | PIS |
| MAY | 5 | ARI |
| JUN | 1 | TAU |
| JUN | 27 | GEM |
| JUL | 22 | CAN |
| AUG | 16 | LEO |
| SEP | 10 | VIR |
| OCT | 4 | LIB |
| OCT | 28 | SCO |
| NOV | 21 | SAG |
| DEC | 14 | CAP |

**1951**

| MTH | DAY | SIGN |
| --- | --- | --- |
| JAN | 1 | CAP |
| JAN | 7 | AQU |
| JAN | 31 | PIS |
| FEB | 24 | ARI |
| MAR | 21 | TAU |
| APR | 15 | GEM |
| MAY | 11 | CAN |
| JUN | 7 | LEO |
| JUL | 8 | VIR |
| NOV | 9 | LIB |
| DEC | 8 | SCO |

**1952**

| MTH | DAY | SIGN |
| --- | --- | --- |
| JAN | 1 | SCO |
| JAN | 2 | SAG |
| JAN | 27 | CAP |
| FEB | 21 | AQU |
| MAR | 16 | PIS |
| APR | 9 | ARI |
| MAY | 4 | TAU |
| MAY | 28 | GEM |
| JUN | 22 | CAN |
| JUL | 16 | LEO |
| AUG | 9 | VIR |
| SEP | 3 | LIB |
| SEP | 27 | SCO |
| OCT | 22 | SAG |
| NOV | 15 | CAP |
| DEC | 10 | AQU |

| | MTH | DAY | SIGN |
|---|---|---|---|
| **1953** | JAN | 1 | AQU |
| | JAN | 5 | PIS |
| | FEB | 2 | ARI |
| | MAR | 14 | TAU |
| | MAR | 31 | ARI |
| | JUN | 5 | TAU |
| | JUL | 7 | GEM |
| | AUG | 4 | CAN |
| | AUG | 30 | LEO |
| | SEP | 24 | VIR |
| | OCT | 18 | LIB |
| | NOV | 11 | SCO |
| | DEC | 5 | SAG |
| | DEC | 29 | CAP |

| | MTH | DAY | SIGN |
|---|---|---|---|
| **1954** | JAN | 1 | CAP |
| | JAN | 22 | AQU |
| | FEB | 15 | PIS |
| | MAR | 11 | ARI |
| | APR | 4 | TAU |
| | APR | 28 | GEM |
| | MAY | 23 | CAN |
| | JUN | 17 | LEO |
| | JUL | 13 | VIR |
| | AUG | 9 | LIB |
| | SEP | 6 | SCO |
| | OCT | 23 | SAG |
| | OCT | 27 | SCO |

| | MTH | DAY | SIGN |
|---|---|---|---|
| **1955** | JAN | 1 | SCO |
| | JAN | 6 | SAG |
| | FEB | 6 | CAP |
| | MAR | 4 | AQU |
| | MAR | 30 | PIS |
| | APR | 24 | ARI |
| | MAY | 19 | TAU |
| | JUN | 13 | GEM |
| | JUL | 8 | CAN |
| | AUG | 1 | LEO |
| | AUG | 25 | VIR |
| | SEP | 18 | LIB |
| | OCT | 13 | SCO |
| | NOV | 6 | SAG |
| | NOV | 30 | CAP |
| | DEC | 24 | AQU |

| | MTH | DAY | SIGN |
|---|---|---|---|
| **1956** | JAN | 1 | AQU |
| | JAN | 17 | PIS |
| | FEB | 11 | ARI |
| | MAR | 7 | TAU |
| | APR | 4 | GEM |
| | MAY | 8 | CAN |
| | JUN | 23 | GEM |
| | AUG | 4 | CAN |
| | SEP | 8 | LEO |
| | OCT | 6 | VIR |
| | OCT | 31 | LIB |
| | NOV | 25 | SCO |
| | DEC | 19 | SAG |

| | MTH | DAY | SIGN |
|---|---|---|---|
| **1957** | JAN | 1 | SAG |
| | JAN | 12 | CAP |
| | FEB | 5 | AQU |
| | MAR | 1 | PIS |
| | MAR | 25 | ARI |
| | APR | 19 | TAU |
| | MAY | 13 | GEM |
| | JUN | 6 | CAN |
| | JUL | 1 | LEO |
| | JUL | 26 | VIR |
| | AUG | 20 | LIB |
| | SEP | 14 | SCO |
| | OCT | 10 | SAG |
| | NOV | 5 | CAP |
| | DEC | 6 | AQU |

| | MTH | DAY | SIGN |
|---|---|---|---|
| **1958** | JAN | 1 | AQU |
| | APR | 6 | PIS |
| | MAY | 5 | ARI |
| | JUN | 1 | TAU |
| | JUN | 26 | GEM |
| | JUL | 22 | CAN |
| | AUG | 16 | LEO |
| | SEP | 9 | VIR |
| | OCT | 3 | LIB |
| | OCT | 27 | SCO |
| | NOV | 20 | SAG |
| | DEC | 14 | CAP |

| | MTH | DAY | SIGN |
|---|---|---|---|
| **1959** | JAN | 1 | CAP |
| | JAN | 7 | AQU |
| | JAN | 31 | PIS |
| | FEB | 24 | ARI |
| | MAR | 20 | TAU |
| | APR | 14 | GEM |
| | MAY | 10 | CAN |
| | JUN | 6 | LEO |
| | JUL | 8 | VIR |
| | SEP | 20 | LEO |
| | SEP | 25 | VIR |
| | NOV | 9 | LIB |
| | DEC | 7 | SCO |

| | MTH | DAY | SIGN |
|---|---|---|---|
| **1960** | JAN | 1 | SCO |
| | JAN | 2 | SAG |
| | JAN | 27 | CAP |
| | FEB | 20 | AQU |
| | MAR | 16 | PIS |
| | APR | 9 | ARI |
| | MAY | 3 | TAU |
| | MAY | 28 | GEM |
| | JUN | 21 | CAN |
| | JUL | 16 | LEO |
| | AUG | 9 | VIR |
| | SEP | 2 | LIB |
| | SEP | 27 | SCO |
| | OCT | 21 | SAG |
| | NOV | 15 | CAP |
| | DEC | 10 | AQU |

## 1961

| MTH | DAY | SIGN |
|-----|-----|------|
| JAN | 1 | AQU |
| JAN | 5 | PIS |
| FEB | 2 | ARI |
| JUN | 5 | TAU |
| JUL | 7 | GEM |
| AUG | 3 | CAN |
| AUG | 29 | LEO |
| SEP | 23 | VIR |
| OCT | 18 | LIB |
| NOV | 11 | SCO |
| DEC | 5 | SAG |
| DEC | 29 | CAP |

## 1962

| MTH | DAY | SIGN |
|-----|-----|------|
| JAN | 1 | CAP |
| JAN | 21 | AQU |
| FEB | 14 | PIS |
| MAR | 10 | ARI |
| APR | 3 | TAU |
| APR | 28 | GEM |
| MAY | 23 | CAN |
| JUN | 17 | LEO |
| JUL | 12 | VIR |
| AUG | 8 | LIB |
| SEP | 7 | SCO |

## 1963

| MTH | DAY | SIGN |
|-----|-----|------|
| JAN | 1 | SCO |
| JAN | 6 | SAG |
| FEB | 5 | CAP |
| MAR | 4 | AQU |
| MAR | 30 | PIS |
| APR | 24 | ARI |
| MAY | 19 | TAU |
| JUN | 12 | GEM |
| JUL | 7 | CAN |
| JUL | 31 | LEO |
| AUG | 25 | VIR |
| SEP | 18 | LIB |
| OCT | 12 | SCO |
| NOV | 5 | SAG |
| NOV | 29 | CAP |
| DEC | 23 | AQU |

## 1964

| MTH | DAY | SIGN |
|-----|-----|------|
| JAN | 1 | AQU |
| JAN | 17 | PIS |
| FEB | 10 | ARI |
| MAR | 7 | TAU |
| APR | 4 | GEM |
| MAY | 9 | CAN |
| JUN | 17 | GEM |
| AUG | 5 | CAN |
| SEP | 8 | LEO |
| OCT | 5 | VIR |
| OCT | 31 | LIB |
| NOV | 25 | SCO |
| DEC | 19 | SAG |

| | MTH | DAY | SIGN | | MTH | DAY | SIGN |
|---|---|---|---|---|---|---|---|
| **1965** | JAN | 1 | SAG | **1966** | JAN | 1 | AQU |
| | JAN | 12 | CAP | | FEB | 6 | CAP |
| | FEB | 5 | AQU | | FEB | 25 | AQU |
| | MAR | 1 | PIS | | APR | 6 | PIS |
| | MAR | 25 | ARI | | MAY | 5 | ARI |
| | APR | 18 | TAU | | MAY | 31 | TAU |
| | MAY | 12 | GEM | | JUN | 26 | GEM |
| | JUN | 6 | CAN | | JUL | 21 | CAN |
| | JUN | 30 | LEO | | AUG | 15 | LEO |
| | JUL | 25 | VIR | | SEP | 8 | VIR |
| | AUG | 19 | LIB | | OCT | 3 | LIB |
| | SEP | 13 | SCO | | OCT | 27 | SCO |
| | OCT | 9 | SAG | | NOV | 20 | SAG |
| | NOV | 5 | CAP | | DEC | 13 | CAP |
| | DEC | 7 | AQU | | | | |

| | MTH | DAY | SIGN | | MTH | DAY | SIGN |
|---|---|---|---|---|---|---|---|
| **1967** | JAN | 1 | CAP | **1968** | JAN | 1 | SAG |
| | JAN | 6 | AQU | | JAN | 26 | CAP |
| | JAN | 30 | PIS | | FEB | 20 | AQU |
| | FEB | 23 | ARI | | MAR | 15 | PIS |
| | MAR | 20 | TAU | | APR | 8 | ARI |
| | APR | 14 | GEM | | MAY | 3 | TAU |
| | MAY | 10 | CAN | | MAY | 27 | GEM |
| | JUN | 6 | LEO | | JUN | 21 | CAN |
| | JUL | 8 | VIR | | JUL | 15 | LEO |
| | SEP | 9 | LEO | | AUG | 8 | VIR |
| | OCT | 1 | VIR | | SEP | 2 | LIB |
| | NOV | 9 | LIB | | SEP | 26 | SCO |
| | DEC | 7 | SCO | | OCT | 21 | SAG |
| | | | | | NOV | 14 | CAP |
| | | | | | DEC | 9 | AQU |

| | MTH | DAY | SIGN |
|---|---|---|---|
| **1969** | JAN | 1 | AQU |
| | JAN | 4 | PIS |
| | FEB | 2 | ARI |
| | JUN | 6 | TAU |
| | JUL | 6 | GEM |
| | AUG | 3 | CAN |
| | SEP | 23 | VIR |
| | OCT | 17 | LIB |
| | NOV | 10 | SCO |
| | DEC | 4 | SAG |
| | DEC | 28 | CAP |

| | MTH | DAY | SIGN |
|---|---|---|---|
| **1970** | JAN | 1 | CAP |
| | JAN | 21 | AQU |
| | FEB | 14 | PIS |
| | MAR | 10 | ARI |
| | APR | 3 | TAU |
| | APR | 27 | GEM |
| | MAY | 22 | CAN |
| | JUN | 16 | LEO |
| | JUL | 12 | VIR |
| | AUG | 8 | LIB |
| | SEP | 7 | SCO |

| | MTH | DAY | SIGN |
|---|---|---|---|
| **1971** | JAN | 1 | SCO |
| | JAN | 7 | SAG |
| | FEB | 5 | CAP |
| | MAR | 4 | AQU |
| | MAR | 29 | PIS |
| | APR | 23 | ARI |
| | MAY | 18 | TAU |
| | JUN | 12 | GEM |
| | JUL | 6 | CAN |
| | JUL | 31 | LEO |
| | AUG | 24 | VIR |
| | SEP | 17 | LIB |
| | OCT | 11 | SCO |
| | NOV | 5 | SAG |
| | NOV | 29 | CAP |
| | DEC | 23 | AQU |

| | MTH | DAY | SIGN |
|---|---|---|---|
| **1972** | JAN | 1 | AQU |
| | JAN | 16 | PIS |
| | FEB | 10 | ARI |
| | MAR | 7 | TAU |
| | APR | 3 | GEM |
| | MAY | 10 | CAN |
| | JUN | 11 | GEM |
| | AUG | 6 | CAN |
| | SEP | 7 | LEO |
| | OCT | 5 | VIR |
| | OCT | 30 | LIB |
| | NOV | 24 | SCO |
| | DEC | 18 | SAG |

| | MTH | DAY | SIGN |
|---|---|---|---|
| **1973** | JAN | 1 | SAG |
| | JAN | 11 | CAP |
| | FEB | 4 | AQU |
| | FEB | 28 | PIS |
| | MAR | 24 | ARI |
| | APR | 18 | TAU |
| | MAY | 12 | GEM |
| | JUN | 5 | CAN |
| | JUN | 30 | LEO |
| | JUL | 25 | VIR |
| | AUG | 19 | LIB |
| | SEP | 13 | SCO |
| | OCT | 9 | SAG |
| | NOV | 5 | CAP |
| | DEC | 7 | AQU |

| | MTH | DAY | SIGN |
|---|---|---|---|
| **1974** | JAN | 1 | AQU |
| | JAN | 29 | CAP |
| | FEB | 28 | AQU |
| | APR | 6 | PIS |
| | MAY | 4 | ARI |
| | MAY | 31 | TAU |
| | JUN | 25 | GEM |
| | JUL | 21 | CAN |
| | AUG | 14 | LEO |
| | SEP | 8 | VIR |
| | OCT | 2 | LIB |
| | OCT | 26 | SCO |
| | NOV | 19 | SAG |
| | DEC | 13 | CAP |

| | MTH | DAY | SIGN |
|---|---|---|---|
| **1975** | JAN | 1 | CAP |
| | JAN | 6 | AQU |
| | JAN | 30 | PIS |
| | FEB | 23 | ARI |
| | MAR | 19 | TAU |
| | APR | 13 | GEM |
| | MAY | 9 | CAN |
| | JUN | 6 | LEO |
| | JUL | 9 | VIR |
| | SEP | 2 | LEO |
| | OCT | 4 | VIR |
| | NOV | 9 | LIB |
| | DEC | 7 | SCO |

| | MTH | DAY | SIGN |
|---|---|---|---|
| **1976** | JAN | 1 | SAG |
| | JAN | 25 | CAP |
| | FEB | 19 | AQU |
| | MAR | 14 | PIS |
| | APR | 7 | ARI |
| | MAY | 2 | TAU |
| | MAY | 27 | GEM |
| | JUN | 20 | CAN |
| | JUL | 14 | LEO |
| | AUG | 7 | VIR |
| | SEP | 1 | LIB |
| | SEP | 25 | SCO |
| | OCT | 20 | SAG |
| | NOV | 14 | CAP |
| | DEC | 9 | AQU |

| | MTH | DAY | SIGN |
|---|---|---|---|
| **1977** | JAN | 1 | AQU |
| | JAN | 4 | PIS |
| | FEB | 2 | ARI |
| | JUN | 6 | TAU |
| | JUL | 6 | GEM |
| | AUG | 2 | CAN |
| | AUG | 28 | LEO |
| | SEP | 22 | VIR |
| | OCT | 17 | LIB |
| | NOV | 10 | SCO |
| | DEC | 4 | SAG |
| | DEC | 27 | CAP |

| | MTH | DAY | SIGN |
|---|---|---|---|
| **1978** | JAN | 1 | CAP |
| | JAN | 20 | AQU |
| | FEB | 13 | PIS |
| | MAR | 9 | ARI |
| | APR | 2 | TAU |
| | APR | 27 | GEM |
| | MAY | 22 | CAN |
| | JUN | 16 | LEO |
| | JUL | 12 | VIR |
| | AUG | 8 | LIB |
| | SEP | 7 | SCO |

| | MTH | DAY | SIGN |
|---|---|---|---|
| **1979** | JAN | 1 | SCO |
| | JAN | 7 | SAG |
| | FEB | 5 | CAP |
| | MAR | 3 | AQU |
| | MAR | 29 | PIS |
| | APR | 23 | ARI |
| | MAY | 18 | TAU |
| | JUN | 11 | GEM |
| | JUL | 6 | CAN |
| | JUL | 30 | LEO |
| | AUG | 24 | VIR |
| | SEP | 17 | LIB |
| | OCT | 11 | SCO |
| | NOV | 4 | SAG |
| | NOV | 28 | CAP |
| | DEC | 22 | AQU |

| | MTH | DAY | SIGN |
|---|---|---|---|
| **1980** | JAN | 1 | AQU |
| | JAN | 16 | PIS |
| | FEB | 9 | ARI |
| | MAR | 6 | TAU |
| | APR | 3 | GEM |
| | MAY | 12 | CAN |
| | JUN | 5 | GEM |
| | AUG | 6 | CAN |
| | SEP | 7 | LEO |
| | OCT | 4 | VIR |
| | OCT | 30 | LIB |
| | NOV | 24 | SCO |
| | DEC | 18 | SAG |

| | MTH | DAY | SIGN |
|---|---|---|---|
| **1981** | JAN | 1 | SAG |
| | JAN | 11 | CAP |
| | FEB | 4 | AQU |
| | FEB | 28 | PIS |
| | MAR | 24 | ARI |
| | APR | 17 | TAU |
| | MAY | 11 | GEM |
| | JUN | 5 | CAN |
| | JUN | 29 | LEO |
| | JUL | 24 | VIR |
| | AUG | 18 | LIB |
| | SEP | 12 | SCO |
| | OCT | 9 | SAG |
| | NOV | 5 | CAP |
| | DEC | 8 | AQU |

| | MTH | DAY | SIGN |
|---|---|---|---|
| **1982** | JAN | 1 | AQU |
| | JAN | 23 | CAP |
| | MAR | 2 | AQU |
| | APR | 6 | PIS |
| | MAY | 4 | ARI |
| | MAY | 30 | TAU |
| | JUN | 25 | GEM |
| | JUL | 20 | CAN |
| | AUG | 14 | LEO |
| | SEP | 7 | VIR |
| | OCT | 2 | LIB |
| | OCT | 26 | SCO |
| | NOV | 18 | SAG |
| | DEC | 12 | CAP |

| | MTH | DAY | SIGN |
|---|---|---|---|
| **1983** | JAN | 1 | CAP |
| | JAN | 5 | AQU |
| | JAN | 29 | PIS |
| | FEB | 22 | ARI |
| | MAR | 19 | TAU |
| | APR | 13 | GEM |
| | MAY | 9 | CAN |
| | JUN | 6 | LEO |
| | JUL | 10 | VIR |
| | AUG | 27 | LEO |
| | OCT | 5 | VIR |
| | NOV | 9 | LIB |
| | DEC | 6 | SCO |

| | MTH | DAY | SIGN |
|---|---|---|---|
| **1984** | JAN | 1 | SAG |
| | JAN | 25 | CAP |
| | FEB | 19 | AQU |
| | MAR | 14 | PIS |
| | APR | 7 | ARI |
| | MAY | 2 | TAU |
| | MAY | 26 | GEM |
| | JUN | 20 | CAN |
| | JUL | 14 | LEO |
| | AUG | 7 | VIR |
| | SEP | 1 | LIB |
| | SEP | 25 | SCO |
| | OCT | 20 | SAG |
| | NOV | 13 | CAP |
| | DEC | 9 | AQU |

# venus in aries

You don't play games, and you don't hang around. If you want to dance someone into bed, you will. If you want to punch someone in the nose, you will. Your style is playful, loud, energetic and oomphy. You're not exactly subtle (how many people have told you that?) but life is too short – and anyway, who cares? It's true that you need a reasonable amount of fire, spark or tension to remain interested in someone. You may be an extreme Venus in Aries type, too, in which case fighting will be part of a relationship pattern. If things settle down and become predictable, you tend to feel uncomfortable. You're not really into cosy coupledom, it's far too boring. The only bigger turn-off is probably wimpy love – the kind that hides behind corners and spends ages making itself obvious. You are out there and up there, and some people love it, and some people loathe it. You like instant results, fast journeys, hot music, loud kissing. You're always six years old, somehow.

**What's in your bedroom?** Boots or trainers, thrown on the floor. Red lipstick.
**Get his horoscope done!** If he's got planets in Aries, Leo or Sagittarius – Ping!

**Get him into bed:** Pretend to arm-wrestle him or pillow-fight him. Yell 'Get out!' and shove him, like Elaine in 'Seinfeld'.
**Women like you:** Chrissie Hynde, Sarah Ferguson, Vivienne Westwood, Lucy from 'Peanuts', Xena the Warrior Princess.

## venus in taurus

You know what's valuable. It may be that antique amethyst ring you bought for a song at a country auction, or the donation you made to the Red Cross last year. You're financially sussed, have an excellent idea of market values, or a strong sense of ethics which goes beyond mere capitalist fluff! You have a good eye for what's beautiful and either appreciate others' artistic talents or have a few yourself. You love the touch of human skin, and heaven is an hour-long massage. You love wool, cotton, velvet. Natural smells and substances. Real flowers, not plastic ones. Your sensuality is highly developed. You love those indulgence days they offer at day spas with champagne, facials and scalp massages thrown in. Money is an issue for you, nonetheless. Luckily you're a born businesswoman or do-it-yourself accountant. Even if you give money to charity, you still know what a loaf of bread costs. Once you find out what you like in life, you stick to it quite stubbornly.

**What's in your bedroom?** One beautiful, valuable object. CDs. Massage oil.
**Get his horoscope done!** If he's got planets in Taurus, Capricorn or Virgo – Great!
**Get him into bed:** Rub his neck or shoulders, let him feel your wool or velvet jacket.
**Women like you:** Paloma Picasso, Barbra Streisand, Enya, Joanna Lumley, Her Majesty the Queen, Janet Jackson, Cher.

## venus in gemini

This side of you is funny and clever. Witty and well-informed. You make the people around you smile, or just laugh, on a daily basis. You don't find it hard to network or make connections – it comes naturally to you, and you enjoy it. You swap business cards, e-mail addresses and phone numbers. You always know what's going on, and who said what to whom (and why). When life becomes too boring, heavy or embarrassing you know how to break it up with exactly the right comment, and people rely on you to do so. Friends, family or lovers make up nicknames for you, or you make up nicknames for them. You read the gossip columns – hell, you could write them. You always put the best comments on people's birthday cards. In your prime, you have run up phone bills bigger than your monthly food budget. You can't stand being bored. You can't cope with bimbos, or himbos. You're brainy and funny, and that's how you get to people. Works every time.

**What's in your bedroom?** Books, magazines, newspapers, telephone, notepad, pens
**Get his horoscope done!** If he's got planets in Gemini, Libra or Aquarius – Ping!
**Get him into bed:** Be smarter than every other woman in the room. Be wittier, too.
**Women like you:** Jennifer Saunders, Ruby Wax, Candice Bergen, Victoria Wood, Nora Ephron (director of *Sleepless in Seattle* and *You've Got Mail*).

## venus in cancer

You're a sweetie, but then you think other people are too. You completely and genuinely care for people, and although you're not a saint, the time and energy you've thrown other people's way qualifies you for minor guru status. You can go too far (you know you can) and not everyone likes emotion or nurturing dripped over them. You make an excellent friend, lover or relative, however. You make people tea, offer them the comfy chair, ask them what's wrong, and give them second helpings of whatever they like. Your other great talent is making your house or flat really feel like a home. It's not just your attention to domestic detail, design, colour or atmosphere. It's because you believe your home is a place to pull people into – a kind of modern-day sanctuary, in fact. You love a family feel. If you can't get it from your own family, you assemble friends around you or create your own family later on. You need a clan around you. You need them, and they need you.

**What's in your bedroom?** Childhood things, gifts from people you love, photographs.
**Get his horoscope done!** If he's got planets in Cancer, Scorpio or Pisces – Ping!
**Get him into bed:** Cluck over him a bit, cuddle him, show cleavage or cook soup.
**Women like you:** Delia Smith, Princess Diana, Hazel

Hawke, Mary Poppins, Kaye Webb (founder of Puffin children's books).

## venus in leo

Lust for life is not your problem. You're into love, good times and creativity in equal amounts, and you have a lot to give in all three areas. Sometimes you live your life like a film, or a television mini-series. You know you do – you can almost watch yourself, watching yourself. Occasionally, everything's just a drama in love. It's better than being bored, though. Some couples are so drab, predictable and ordinary they make you want to hurl yourself off the balcony. Little scenes are not uncommon with you, in love, at work, with friends, or with the family. You also like being around people and events with a bit of an ooh-ah-wow factor. You need a man you can link arms with and look good with. Is it his talent, job, looks, cash or reputation? You adore luxury. You don't care about saving money; you'd rather have Chanel, Prada or The Ritz every time.

**What's in your bedroom?** The kinds of little luxuries Hollywood stars and English royals probably get for Christmas.

**Get his horoscope done!** If he's got planets in Aries, Leo or Sagittarius – Ping!

**Get him into bed:** Turn it into a little saga, give it a bit of style, suspense or drama.

**Women like you:** Coco Chanel, Jacqueline Kennedy Onassis, Courtney Love, Madonna, Lady Penelope, Nancy Mitford.

## venus in virgo

If a job's worth doing, it's worth doing perfectly well. You love the details of the work you do, or the papers you pile up on the desk. Getting it right, in a precise and perfect way, is extremely satisfying. Others jam the last piece of the jigsaw into place and make it fit. It looks ugly, and you hate that. You patiently sort and file until you find the right piece, and then . . . perfection. Sex can be like that with you, too. It's nice if it's down to a precision art sometimes. You also get a lot from helping people and quietly doing things for them in a practical way. If you love a man, you probably can't help him enough. If it's a work thing as well, then even better. You understand. You don't mind getting involved – after all, if there's one thing you appreciate, it's the all-nature of work. Because you want perfection so much, in so many ways, you can get too picky, too critical, and too analytical with the poor old human beings around you – and yourself. It doesn't have to be like that, though. You love a routine, and most Venus in Virgo women have little daily rules and rituals about healthy eating and drinking.

**What's in your bedroom?** A clean smell, and crisp bedlinen. A definite absence of dust.

**Get his horoscope done!** If he's got planets in Taurus, Virgo or Capricorn – Ping!

**Get him into bed:** Ask him about his work, offer him a practical piece of help or a useful favour.

**Women like you:** Miss Moneypenny (James Bond's PA), Claudia Schiffer, Shirley Conran, Lois Lane.

## venus in libra

You know what looks good, and if it doesn't look good, you're probably too nice to say anything, but you quietly die inside. This applies to clothes, houses, art . . . you name it. Your ears are also sensitive (which may reveal itself during sex) and music moves you. You're a mirror-hopper. If you're going out somewhere important and you're not quite sure about the shoes, or the hair, or the jacket (how many times has that happened?), you hop from mirror to mirror throughout the evening. Other people don't notice – they're too busy being charmed by you. You can turn it on, and that's okay. Some people race towards conversational crashes, but you spot the danger zone ten kilometres before it happens and smoothly swerve everything away from the trouble-spot. Born with this Venus sign, you can truly never get enough of love and romance. In your own life, in other people's lives, in films, in poems, in endless re-runs of 'Pride and Prejudice' on TV . . . You crave the balance that comes when people can be peaceful with each other. That's true beauty. And you love a true working partnership, either in your career or your private life. You especially enjoy it when you balance someone else out with your differences, and vice versa.

**What's in your bedroom?** Photographs or paintings. Wardrobe contents to die for.
**Get his horoscope done!** Has he got planets in Gemini, Libra or Aquarius? Ping!
**Get him into bed:** Send him flowers. Do something old-fashioned and girlie; wear lace or roses.
**Women like you:** Dawn French, Jayne Torvill, Olivia Newton-John, Linda McCartney, Susan Sarandon.

*You're a Scorpio with Venus in Libra*
You'll bounce off people whose Star Signs or Venus Signs
are Libra and Gemini. And sometimes you'll do more
than just bounce!

# venus in scorpio

People never tell you what nice weather we're having, because they sense something in your eyes that would kill them at five paces. You were made for more than polite conversation or meaningless social crapola. You are an extremely intense, emotional and passionate woman. Relationships bring it out, like the sun luring a tiger snake from its burrow. You go very, very deep with people. The love is several hundred leagues below the sea; the sex resonates inside a dark and moist echo chamber; the hatred (well, you *do* hate) is earthquake-level. Other people like boring happy endings. You tend not to believe in them. You know about the blood, tears, sweat, vomit, rage, pain, ecstasy and orgasmic highs instead. You dig deeply into life, and it sometimes digs back. You can carry too much poison, and you know it. But nobody understands human nature better. You could write a book about sex, alone. But you never would. You're far too private. Sometimes only really passionate music or poetry can contain and express the enormous power and depth of your emotions, especially where love is concerned.

**What's in your bedroom?** Black lingerie, dim lights, intense novels about sex, death, power, the occult or revenge.

**Get his horoscope done!** Does he have planets in Cancer, Scorpio or Pisces? Ping!

**Get him into bed:** Scorch his pants off with your eyes. Lick your lips and look away a lot.

**Women like you:** Marianne Faithfull, k.d. lang, Demi Moore, Julia Roberts, Anne Rice, Cruella De Vil (when you have PMT).

*You're a Scorpio with Venus in Scorpio*
Some of your strongest friendships and relationships will be with people whose Star Signs or Venus Signs are Scorpio, Cancer or Pisces.

## venus in sagittarius

You know what and who you believe in, and it could be anything from a philosophy of life you've made up yourself to something more formal – like reincarnation, or heaven and hell, or socialism. You have your code, and that's it. Occasionally people get a free lecture, but you mean well. You're funny, or can appreciate other people being funny. You need to have adventures in your life, or to go exploring, to really feel as if you're following your heart. Staying stuck in a rut for security's sake is not you. As you get older, the search for a sense of meaning, and for meaningful relationships, matters more. You don't like the idea that the world is some big, random place. You're always looking for the true explanation, no matter if it's religious, cosmic, scientific or spiritual. When you were younger, you typically fooled around, horsed around and fell out of bed a lot. You really adore travel, and people from other countries. The day you discover hotmail (www.hotmail.com on the Internet) is the day you discover pure heaven. How many friends or potential lovers in how many countries can you actually have?

**What's in your bedroom?** A travel bag that still hasn't been fully unpacked. Travel books or brochures.
**Get his horoscope done!** Has he got planets in Aries, Leo or Sagittarius? Ping!
**Get him into bed:** Tell him a joke, exaggerate a story, rave about your favourite place in the world.

**Women like you:** Bette Midler, Kaz Cooke, Meg Ryan, Karen Blixen, Maggie O'Connell in 'Northern Exposure'.

*You're a Scorpio with Venus in Sagittarius*
The fiery side of your personality will produce a definite 'click' with people who have Sagittarius or Aries Star Signs or Venus Signs.

## venus in capricorn

There is a part of you that is so solid, so grounded, so normal and so sensible that people could drug you, dress you up in floppy bunny ears and spin you around, and you'd still seem worryingly sane and down to earth. You are particularly serious about love and relationships. It can cause you pain, but you are wise enough to know that pain is just another word for experience, and you can't have a mature or seasoned relationship without it. You like to know where you stand, basically. This philosophy guides you in love, in life and in most things you enjoy. What's the story? You have an inbuilt wanker detector, which is why the more insane Paris fashions leave you cold, and people with pretensions turn you off. You're not particularly spontaneous or outrageous, but that's okay. Like-minded people find you eventually, and that's basically what you're after. You love success, no matter whether it's scoring points at the coolest function in town, or pulling off an amazing career coup.

**What's in your bedroom?** Bits and pieces from work, old or antique things.
**Get his horoscope done!** Does he have planets in Taurus, Virgo or Capricorn? Ping!
**Get him into bed:** Play by the rules of the situation, keep your dignity, be cool about it.
**Women like you:** Sharon Stone, Maggie Tabberer, Cindy Crawford, Tess McGill in *Working Girl*.

## venus in aquarius

You love people and ideas which are alternative, different or out there. You're instinctively drawn to astrology, for example. You may also enjoy the Internet. You love your network of friends, and you have a lot of them – nothing too emotional, close or complicated, though. You certainly don't have a problem with platonic male–female friendships. Where love is concerned, you appreciate a relationship where you both have your own space and independence.

If it feels cool, free, intelligent, feminist and progressive, then you'll go for it. You have unusual tastes and interests by other people's standards, and your wardrobe, home or haircut might reflect this. You can live with uncertainty and weirdness in your love life if it means you still get electricity and excitement. When you go to an art gallery or a shopping plaza you tend to find yourself preferring the bits and pieces nobody else likes – either that or you just walk out!

**What's in your bedroom?** Things that are in no other woman's bedroom on Earth.

**Get his horoscope done!** Has he got planets in Gemini, Libra or Aquarius? Ping!

**Get him into bed:** Be original, be cool, be different, be yourself, shock him a bit.

**Women like you:** Dame Edna Everage, Germaine Greer, Kate Bush, Gloria Steinem, Lieutenant Uhura in 'Star Trek'.

## venus in pisces

You can take emotional or physical pain away from people and animals, and that's a good thing. If you couldn't do that, you'd probably have to crawl away somewhere. You are so intensely sensitive – not only in terms of your own head-space, but also other people's – that you bruise very easily. There are two ways around this. Either you can soothe suffering away, or you simply have to escape. It doesn't have to involve a lot of money; sometimes all you have to do is daydream, or light some incense. A complete fantasy voyage is something you periodically need to spend money on, though. Your imagination and your idealism are strong, and can get you into serious trouble with men. Sometimes the fact that you wear blinkers is a lovely thing, as it lets you accept men with all their faults and still love them. At other times you can almost feel crucified over it. A bit of balance in your life is a good thing. Poetry, art, photography or music are superb channels. You may also be drawn to the spiritual or psychic side of life.

**What's in your bedroom?** Impractical but intensely wonderful objects. Fabulous fabrics. Arty photographs.
**Get his horoscope done!** Does he have planets in Cancer, Scorpio, Pisces? Ping!
**Get him into bed:** Read his mind in a sympathetic way. Flutter your fingers on his arm.

**Women like you:** Neneh Cherry, Joy Adamson,
Elizabeth Taylor, Jilly Cooper, Anaïs Nin, The Little
Mermaid.

# six

# profile of your soulmate

Look up your date and year of birth in the tables to find out your soulmate profile. For example, if you were born on 6 January 1960, when Mars was in the sign of Sagittarius, your soulmate is an explorer; if you were born on 16 January 1960, after Mars had moved into Capricorn, then your soulmate is an achiever. If your birthday falls outside the years shown in these tables, check out www.astro.com on the Internet — it'll give you a free run-down of all your planets.

No matter when your birthday is, though, there are certain qualities you will always identify with in men. Because you are a Scorpio, some of your ideas about what a 'real' man is are based on your Star Sign. He has to be quite deep, particularly on an emotional level, for a start. He'll have to have an intense quality, and that in-depth gaze that's the mark of the true obsessive. Men who are too superficial or lightweight may not really seem like 'true' men to you. Chances are, your ex-boyfriends or your current partner will have some of these qualities:

- A secretive side
- A sexy, relentless, almost fanatical approach to his job, his interests – or you
- A strong survival instinct
- An instinct for sex, and everything that it involves.

To discover the sort of man who really is a part of you, though, explore this next section. Add these qualities to the traits you've just read about, and you'll begin to get an accurate picture of your astrological soulmate.

**1949**

| MTH | DAY | SIGN |
|-----|-----|------|
| JAN | 1 | CAP |
| JAN | 4 | AQU |
| FEB | 11 | PIS |
| MAR | 21 | ARI |
| APR | 30 | TAU |
| JUN | 10 | GEM |
| JUL | 23 | CAN |
| SEP | 7 | LEO |
| OCT | 27 | VIR |
| DEC | 26 | LIB |

**1950**

| MTH | DAY | SIGN |
|-----|-----|------|
| JAN | 1 | LIB |
| MAR | 28 | VIR |
| JUN | 11 | LIB |
| AUG | 10 | SCO |
| SEP | 25 | SAG |
| NOV | 6 | CAP |
| DEC | 15 | AQU |

**1951**

| MTH | DAY | SIGN |
|-----|-----|------|
| JAN | 1 | AQU |
| JAN | 22 | PIS |
| MAR | 1 | ARI |
| APR | 10 | TAU |
| MAY | 21 | GEM |
| JUL | 3 | CAN |
| AUG | 18 | LEO |
| OCT | 5 | VIR |
| NOV | 24 | LIB |

**1952**

| MTH | DAY | SIGN |
|-----|-----|------|
| JAN | 1 | LIB |
| JAN | 20 | SCO |
| AUG | 27 | SAG |
| OCT | 12 | CAP |
| NOV | 21 | AQU |
| DEC | 30 | PIS |

**1953**

| MTH | DAY | SIGN |
|-----|-----|------|
| JAN | 1 | PIS |
| FEB | 8 | ARI |
| MAR | 20 | TAU |
| MAY | 1 | GEM |
| JUN | 14 | CAN |
| JUL | 29 | LEO |
| SEP | 14 | VIR |
| NOV | 1 | LIB |
| DEC | 20 | SCO |

**1954**

| MTH | DAY | SIGN |
|-----|-----|------|
| JAN | 1 | SCO |
| FEB | 9 | SAG |
| APR | 12 | CAP |
| JUL | 3 | SAG |
| AUG | 24 | CAP |
| OCT | 21 | AQU |
| DEC | 4 | PIS |

**1955**

| MTH | DAY | SIGN |
|-----|-----|------|
| JAN | 1 | PIS |
| JAN | 15 | ARI |
| FEB | 26 | TAU |
| APR | 10 | GEM |
| MAY | 26 | CAN |
| JUL | 11 | LEO |
| AUG | 27 | VIR |
| OCT | 13 | LIB |
| NOV | 29 | SCO |

**1956**

| MTH | DAY | SIGN |
|-----|-----|------|
| JAN | 1 | SCO |
| JAN | 14 | SAG |
| FEB | 28 | CAP |
| APR | 14 | AQU |
| JUN | 3 | PIS |
| DEC | 6 | ARI |

**1957**

| MTH | DAY | SIGN |
|-----|-----|------|
| JAN | 1 | ARI |
| JAN | 28 | TAU |
| MAR | 17 | GEM |
| MAY | 4 | CAN |
| JUN | 21 | LEO |
| AUG | 8 | VIR |
| SEP | 24 | LIB |
| NOV | 8 | SCO |
| DEC | 23 | SAG |

**1958**

| MTH | DAY | SIGN |
|-----|-----|------|
| JAN | 1 | SAG |
| FEB | 3 | CAP |
| MAR | 17 | AQU |
| APR | 27 | PIS |
| JUN | 7 | ARI |
| JUL | 21 | TAU |
| SEP | 21 | GEM |
| OCT | 29 | TAU |

**1959**

| MTH | DAY | SIGN |
|-----|-----|------|
| JAN | 1 | TAU |
| FEB | 10 | GEM |
| APR | 10 | CAN |
| JUN | 1 | LEO |
| JUL | 20 | VIR |
| SEP | 5 | LIB |
| OCT | 21 | SCO |
| DEC | 3 | SAG |

**1960**

| MTH | DAY | SIGN |
|-----|-----|------|
| JAN | 1 | SAG |
| JAN | 14 | CAP |
| FEB | 23 | AQU |
| APR | 2 | PIS |
| MAY | 11 | ARI |
| JUN | 20 | TAU |
| AUG | 2 | GEM |
| SEP | 21 | CAN |

## 1961

| MTH | DAY | SIGN |
|-----|-----|------|
| JAN | 1 | CAN |
| FEB | 5 | GEM |
| FEB | 7 | CAN |
| MAY | 6 | LEO |
| JUN | 28 | VIR |
| AUG | 17 | LIB |
| OCT | 1 | SCO |
| NOV | 13 | SAG |
| DEC | 24 | CAP |

## 1962

| MTH | DAY | SIGN |
|-----|-----|------|
| JAN | 1 | CAP |
| FEB | 1 | AQU |
| MAR | 12 | PIS |
| APR | 19 | ARI |
| MAY | 28 | TAU |
| JUL | 9 | GEM |
| AUG | 22 | CAN |
| OCT | 11 | LEO |

## 1963

| MTH | DAY | SIGN |
|-----|-----|------|
| JAN | 1 | LEO |
| JUN | 3 | VIR |
| JUL | 27 | LIB |
| SEP | 12 | SCO |
| OCT | 25 | SAG |
| DEC | 5 | CAP |

## 1964

| MTH | DAY | SIGN |
|-----|-----|------|
| JAN | 1 | CAP |
| JAN | 13 | AQU |
| FEB | 20 | PIS |
| MAR | 29 | ARI |
| MAY | 7 | TAU |
| JUN | 17 | GEM |
| JUL | 30 | CAN |
| SEP | 15 | LEO |
| NOV | 6 | VIR |

## 1965

| MTH | DAY | SIGN |
|-----|-----|------|
| JAN | 1 | VIR |
| JUN | 29 | LIB |
| AUG | 20 | SCO |
| OCT | 4 | SAG |
| NOV | 14 | CAP |
| DEC | 23 | AQU |

## 1966

| MTH | DAY | SIGN |
|-----|-----|------|
| JAN | 1 | AQU |
| JAN | 30 | PIS |
| MAR | 9 | ARI |
| APR | 17 | TAU |
| MAY | 28 | GEM |
| JUL | 11 | CAN |
| AUG | 25 | LEO |
| OCT | 12 | VIR |
| DEC | 4 | LIB |

## 1967

| MTH | DAY | SIGN |
|-----|-----|------|
| JAN | 1 | LIB |
| FEB | 12 | SCO |
| MAR | 31 | LIB |
| JUL | 19 | SCO |
| SEP | 10 | SAG |
| OCT | 23 | CAP |
| DEC | 1 | AQU |

## 1968

| MTH | DAY | SIGN |
|-----|-----|------|
| JAN | 1 | AQU |
| JAN | 9 | PIS |
| FEB | 17 | ARI |
| MAR | 27 | TAU |
| MAY | 8 | GEM |
| JUN | 21 | CAN |
| AUG | 5 | LEO |
| SEP | 21 | VIR |
| NOV | 9 | LIB |
| DEC | 29 | SCO |

## 1969

| MTH | DAY | SIGN |
|-----|-----|------|
| JAN | 1 | SCO |
| FEB | 25 | SAG |
| SEP | 21 | CAP |
| NOV | 4 | AQU |
| DEC | 15 | PIS |

## 1970

| MTH | DAY | SIGN |
|-----|-----|------|
| JAN | 1 | PIS |
| JAN | 24 | ARI |
| MAR | 7 | TAU |
| APR | 18 | GEM |
| JUN | 2 | CAN |
| JUL | 18 | LEO |
| SEP | 3 | VIR |
| OCT | 20 | LIB |
| DEC | 6 | SCO |

## 1971

| MTH | DAY | SIGN |
|-----|-----|------|
| JAN | 1 | SCO |
| JAN | 23 | SAG |
| MAR | 12 | CAP |
| MAY | 3 | AQU |
| NOV | 6 | PIS |
| DEC | 26 | ARI |

## 1972

| MTH | DAY | SIGN |
|-----|-----|------|
| JAN | 1 | ARI |
| FEB | 10 | TAU |
| MAR | 27 | GEM |
| MAY | 12 | CAN |
| JUN | 28 | LEO |
| AUG | 15 | VIR |
| SEP | 30 | LIB |
| NOV | 15 | SCO |
| DEC | 30 | SAG |

### 1973

| MTH | DAY | SIGN |
|-----|-----|------|
| JAN | 1 | SAG |
| FEB | 12 | CAP |
| MAR | 26 | AQU |
| MAY | 8 | PIS |
| JUN | 20 | ARI |
| AUG | 12 | TAU |
| OCT | 29 | ARI |
| DEC | 24 | TAU |

### 1974

| MTH | DAY | SIGN |
|-----|-----|------|
| JAN | 1 | TAU |
| FEB | 27 | GEM |
| APR | 20 | CAN |
| JUN | 9 | LEO |
| JUL | 27 | VIR |
| SEP | 12 | LIB |
| OCT | 28 | SCO |
| DEC | 10 | SAG |

### 1975

| MTH | DAY | SIGN |
|-----|-----|------|
| JAN | 1 | SAG |
| JAN | 21 | CAP |
| MAR | 3 | AQU |
| APR | 11 | PIS |
| MAY | 21 | ARI |
| JUL | 1 | TAU |
| AUG | 14 | GEM |
| OCT | 17 | CAN |
| NOV | 25 | GEM |

### 1976

| MTH | DAY | SIGN |
|-----|-----|------|
| JAN | 1 | GEM |
| MAR | 18 | CAN |
| MAY | 15 | LEO |
| JUL | 7 | VIR |
| AUG | 4 | LIB |
| OCT | 9 | SCO |
| NOV | 21 | SAG |
| DEC | 12 | CAP |

### 1977

| MTH | DAY | SIGN |
|-----|-----|------|
| JAN | 1 | CAP |
| FEB | 9 | AQU |
| MAR | 20 | PIS |
| APR | 27 | ARI |
| JUN | 6 | TAU |
| JUL | 17 | GEM |
| SEP | 1 | CAN |
| OCT | 26 | LEO |

### 1978

| MTH | DAY | SIGN |
|-----|-----|------|
| JAN | 1 | LEO |
| JAN | 26 | CAN |
| APR | 10 | LEO |
| JUN | 14 | VIR |
| AUG | 4 | LIB |
| SEP | 19 | SCO |
| NOV | 2 | SAG |
| DEC | 12 | CAP |

| MTH | DAY | SIGN |
|-----|-----|------|
| JAN | 1 | CAP |
| JAN | 20 | AQU |
| FEB | 27 | PIS |
| APR | 7 | ARI |
| MAY | 16 | TAU |
| JUN | 26 | GEM |
| AUG | 8 | CAN |
| SEP | 24 | LEO |
| NOV | 19 | VIR |

**1979**

| MTH | DAY | SIGN |
|-----|-----|------|
| JAN | 1 | VIR |
| MAR | 11 | LEO |
| MAY | 4 | VIR |
| JUL | 10 | LIB |
| AUG | 29 | SCO |
| OCT | 12 | SAG |
| NOV | 22 | CAP |
| DEC | 30 | AQU |

**1980**

| MTH | DAY | SIGN |
|-----|-----|------|
| JAN | 1 | AQU |
| FEB | 6 | PIS |
| MAR | 17 | ARI |
| APR | 25 | TAU |
| JUN | 5 | GEM |
| JUL | 18 | CAN |
| SEP | 2 | LEO |
| OCT | 21 | VIR |
| DEC | 16 | LIB |

**1981**

| MTH | DAY | SIGN |
|-----|-----|------|
| JAN | 1 | LIB |
| AUG | 3 | SCO |
| SEP | 20 | SAG |
| OCT | 31 | CAP |
| DEC | 10 | AQU |

**1982**

| MTH | DAY | SIGN |
|-----|-----|------|
| JAN | 1 | AQU |
| JAN | 17 | PIS |
| FEB | 25 | ARI |
| APR | 5 | TAU |
| MAY | 16 | GEM |
| JUN | 29 | CAN |
| AUG | 13 | LEO |
| SEP | 30 | VIR |
| NOV | 18 | LIB |

**1983**

| MTH | DAY | SIGN |
|-----|-----|------|
| JAN | 1 | LIB |
| JAN | 11 | SCO |
| AUG | 17 | SAG |
| OCT | 5 | CAP |
| NOV | 15 | AQU |
| DEC | 25 | PIS |

**1984**

| You have . . . | Your soulmate is a . . . |
| --- | --- |
| Mars in Aries | ✲ go-getter |
| Mars in Taurus | ✲ rock |
| Mars in Gemini | ✲ communicator |
| Mars in Cancer | ✲ caretaker |
| Mars in Leo | ✲ star |
| Mars in Virgo | ✲ thinker |
| Mars in Libra | ✲ balancer |
| Mars in Scorpio | ✲ depth charge |
| Mars in Sagittarius | ✲ explorer |
| Mars in Capricorn | ✲ achiever |
| Mars in Aquarius | ✲ individual |
| Mars in Pisces | ✲ dreamer |

## go-getter

✲ **Let's face it:** He has drive and energy. He's an action man, either at work, or on the weekends. He has loads of initiative. He's not afraid of people or situations which might intimidate other people. He can't survive without challenges to keep him going. He's masculine, in the old-fashioned sense of the word. He never gives up, or gives in. He doesn't hang around. He doesn't waste any time. In a word, he has balls. He'll never walk away from a fight or an argument – backing down makes him feel sick.

✻ **Why you'll love this side of him:** It's a turn-on, basically. He had the wimp part of his brain extracted before he was born. You'll know exactly what's going on with him, because he's in or out of situations so quickly. His male energy is extremely sexy.

✻ **Why you'll loathe this side of him:** He's incredibly pushy. Why doesn't he just let up sometimes? He can be an absolute bastard in an argument. He lacks patience and sensitivity just when you need it most. He basically puts himself first – all too often.

✻ **What you tell your friends:** 'He doesn't waste any time.'

## rock

✻ **Let's face it:** He calms you down. He's so down to earth about life. No pretensions. No wanky ideas about things. He takes his time. He makes life seem settled and normal. He brings in the money, or puts up the shelves, or sorts out the garden. He's

like a good massage at the end of a stressful day.
He understands money, but he also has a straight
sense of ethics, morals and values. He appreciates
fine workmanship and beautiful places and objects.

✵ **Why you'll love this side of him:** He's soothing
company. He's in no hurry. There is something
concrete, solid and secure about him. He has
money in the bank, his own home, or a stable
lifestyle. When he tells you that you're looking
good, you know it's true.

✵ **Why you'll loathe this side of him:** He can be the
world's most boring plodder. He can get stuck in a rut
and keep you there too. He can be so into money,
houses, business or possessions that you wonder if
there's more to life. He's too swayed by appearances.

✵ **What you tell your friends:** 'He's nice and he's
normal.'

## communicator

✵ **Let's face it:** You'll never be bored. He's quick on
the uptake. He's funny too. And he gives great
phone, writes the best letters, and lends you
amazing books. He's scarily intelligent, and he can

make you laugh when life gets too heavy or serious.
He can usually tell you the latest news headlines,
or at least the latest dirt on people. He's a mine of
information, but he's never dull about it. He's fast
and sharp, well-informed and a natural reader,
writer, talker or thinker.

❋ **Why you'll love this side of him:** He's
entertaining. He actually applies his brain to things,
and you'll either want to tape-record the phone
messages or save the love letters in a bank safe.
You can imagine him being switched on, funny and
intelligent at the age of 70.

❋ **Why you'll loathe this side of him:** When he
stops being clever about everything, he just sounds
totally superficial and shallow. And there are times
when you wish he would switch off his whirring
brain and feel something with a bit more true soul.

❋ **What you tell your friends:** 'Let me read you
what he put on my Valentine's Day card.'

## caretaker

❋ **Let's face it:** He turns houses or flats into real
homes. He has a good, strong relationship with at

least one family member — maybe more. It's part of the reason he has such a caring nature. He doesn't waste money. But even so, he's into people — not things. He can be sweet and sympathetic, like a human Band-aid. He's walking proof that you don't have to be a SNAG (Sensitive New Age Guy) in order to be sensitive. He actually cares.

✲ **Why you'll love this side of him:** He's even sweet when he sulks. He knows why families are important, and takes children or parenthood seriously, whether he's into it or not. He's extremely emotional, and he's more in touch with his feelings than other men.

✲ **Why you'll loathe this side of him:** He can become overly attached to one of four things — his home, his mother, his country or his family. To you, it just looks like he's clinging to something. His irrational moods and feelings are all emotion and no brains.

✲ **What you tell your friends:** 'He'd make a great father.'

## star

✲ **Let's face it:** He is respected and admired. He is a legend in his own lunchtime — and a few other people's. He has strong leadership qualities or powerful self-expression. As a result of this, he tends to shine – and also to stand out. He doesn't lack confidence. In fact, his ego sometimes blows out. He has what it takes to tell other people what to do. He may also have the ability to create, perform or entertain. He has style. He has class.

- **Why you'll love this side of him:** He's special. A leader of men, or even slightly famous. Everyone's heard of him. You respect him. He makes you look good. He's the kind of man you can genuinely look up to. And he doesn't have a confidence problem – thank God.
- **Why you'll loathe this side of him:** He can be so arrogant you want to walk out on him. And the drama! He can turn the smallest thing into a three-act play. He's quite self-involved, and wants the bathroom mirror when you do. And – yes – he can be a wanker.
- **What you tell your friends:** 'He's not short on confidence.'

# thinker

✵ **Let's face it:** He's efficient and smart. He has his home life or work life sorted out. Part of it's down to the fact that he's always making lists. But he also finds it easy to get his head around things. He's smart, he's sussed. He doesn't boast about it, but he has the kind of brain that computers will never copy. He's helpful. He's reliable. You know where you are with him. He takes care of his health. He's completely responsible.

✵ **Why you'll love this side of him:** He's very careful and methodical, which you like to see in a man. He takes good care of his body, his workplace and his life. He's sorted. He's impressively intelligent. If you've been with drifters or dreamers, he's the antidote.

✵ **Why you'll loathe this side of him:** He can be ridiculously picky and critical, taking one detail about you, or your behaviour, or your life, and treating it like a major problem. He can be irritatingly boring about the small details of life, fussing around with trivial things.

✵ **What you tell your friends:** 'He's totally reliable.'

# balancer

✵ **Let's face it:** He is very good at keeping your relationship evenly balanced, and will usually compromise to avoid an argument. If you ever actually fight, he won't have a problem with making the peace. His taste in clothes, music, art or homes is very important to him. He is naturally quite charming and diplomatic with people, and he's safe to take anywhere, from your parents' place to a rave. He has a talent for getting on with people – and for relationships.

✵ **Why you'll love this side of him:** He believes in flowers, and he actually watches the close-up scenes in romantic films. He can relate to *Romeo and Juliet*. He cares about the way he dresses and how he gets his hair cut. He also appreciates your style or taste.

✵ **Why you'll loathe this side of him:** This man can be the original fence-sitter, never actually expressing an opinion in case it makes him unpopular with someone. Sometimes he can seem fake, especially on a social level. Charm is fine, but he can take it too far.

✿ **What you tell your friends:** 'Guess what he did for my birthday!'

## depth charge

✿ **Let's face it:** He's a passionate man. He feels things very deeply, and is intense about what and who he loves – and what and who he hates! He has quite a bit of power or magnetism about him. And sexually, inane terms like 'shagging' or 'bonking' don't apply. Sex is not trivial to him. It's about a deep, emotional and powerful connection which goes way beyond the physical. He's a fairly secretive, closed person. That can be quite sexy too.

✿ **Why you'll love this side of him:** He's got soul. He's not a boy, he's a man. He burns for things, and you love it. He truly understands life in all its gory detail, and doesn't mind facing extreme situations or emotions with you. He's a powerful and influential person.

✿ **Why you'll loathe this side of him:** His dark side is ten times as black as any other man's. He can be manipulative – a real power tripper, in fact. It may come out at work, or (worst-case scenario) in his

private life. He can be ridiculously obsessive
about things.

☼ **What you tell your friends:** 'Sex with him is . . .'

## explorer

☼ **Let's face it:** He's into the big picture. He likes
travelling to other countries, or exploring the great
outdoors, or getting out of the house and into more
interesting experiences. He's funny, too – his sense
of humour is healthy. There is nothing narrow-
minded or petty about this bloke. He has the long
view of life. He's a bit of a philosopher at heart.
He's also drawn to friendships with travellers,
foreigners or people who've studied quite widely.

☼ **Why you'll love this side of him:** You could have
a lot of fun taking off to Asia, Europe or America
together. He's game for most things. He has the
right angle on life, too. He never takes it too
seriously. His horizons are broader than most
men's, and that's sexy.

☼ **Why you'll loathe this side of him:** You'd
probably prefer it if he spent less time gazing at the
next horizon, and a little more time on the small

stuff – like security, intimacy, your feelings, and all the practical details of life. And sometimes his jokes aren't funny.

- **What you tell your friends:** 'He has the most amazing attitude towards life.'

## achiever

- **Let's face it:** He's a heavyweight. He's more mature than a lot of the guys around him, and he's got a wise, sussed, experienced quality. No wonder his career to date has been such a success story. He's prepared to wait for what he wants. And he's also prepared to work hard. He's straight-up and serious, and that can be quite sexy, because you will instinctively feel like getting him to loosen up – preferably in bed.
- **Why you'll love this side of him:** There's a lot to admire about this man. He gets to the top by doing things the old-fashioned way. He has a lot of wisdom and experience, and that's something you can respect. He makes you feel safe. You know where you stand.
- **Why you'll loathe this side of him:** His

ambitions – both in career terms and socially – are
quite high. You could get awfully sick of watching
his social game-playing with 'useful' people, or
hearing about work politics. You might find he's
hung up on status too.

☼ **What you tell your friends:** 'He's got it together.'

## individual

☼ **Let's face it:** He's one of a kind. He's not very
good at fitting in for the sake of it. He might look
different from other people, or just be extremely
different on the inside. He's exciting to be around.
You'll feel a definite buzz when you're with him.
He's also a man ahead of his time, in many ways.
What he's into now, everyone else will be into next
year. He doesn't fake it, or compromise. He's his
own person, and he's an absolute original.

☼ **Why you'll love this side of him:** He's very broad-
minded and progressive about life. He understands
feminism and has a basically decent, admirable,
humanitarian view of the world. He's electrifying
company. And he has a dash of genius.

☼ **Why you'll loathe this side of him:** Mad, mad,

mad. Sometimes he can be so stubbornly different
and weird. If you go left, he'll go right. If
everyone's going north, he'll go south. You feel like
kicking him! Then there are his funny little ways –
they're not always funny.

✤ **What you tell your friends:** 'He's one of a kind.'

## dreamer

✤ **Let's face it:** He's sensitive. He's raw like sushi.
He is emotional or psychic, or both at the same
time. He can relate to music, poetry, photography or
films in a profound way because of this sensitivity.
He's not afraid to make sacrifices for other people.
And you don't have to explain how you're feeling to
him – he just seems to know instinctively. He can't
handle too much reality. He needs to drift off,
dream or escape.

✤ **Why you'll love this side of him:** At last, a man
with feelings! He's hard to catch or pin down
sometimes, but like a half-remembered song,
you'll be happily haunted by him. He's kind and
compassionate. He can feel for a hurt woman,
or a hurt butterfly. He's soft inside.

* **Why you'll loathe this side of him:** You know
that song, 'Reality Used To Be A Friend Of Mine'?
You can probably relate to it if you're with this guy.
Drink or drugs may not bring out the best in him.
But his worst faults are vagueness, hopelessness
and chaotic life mess!

* **What you tell your friends:** 'He feels what I'm
feeling.'

# seven

## the spooky bit at the back

Over the years, my job as an astrologer has given me the chance to explore other New Age ideas as well. Some of them work, some of them don't. I met Shirley MacLaine once. I asked her if there was anything in the New Age she didn't believe. She shook her head and said she believed in *everything*. I don't. But here are some quick tips and spooky solutions that I've road-tested over the last ten years. They've got nothing to do with astrology, but they really work!

## feng shui your bedroom

Have you been waiting on money for months? Is someone at work driving you insane? Do you want to go to Morocco but have no idea how you'll manage it? Try feng shui (say it 'fong-shoy').

You can feng shui your whole house or flat if you wish, but for a quick fix, begin with your bedroom. The first thing you will need to do is get rid of any mess, junk or unwanted objects. Here are some classic examples:

- *Clothes that need mending that you've shoved under the bed*
- *Dead or dying plants*
- *Photos of ex-boyfriends, old letters, receipts, bills and other bits of paper*
- *Compact discs or tapes you never play*
- *Magazines and newspapers*
- *Books you've never got around to reading*
- *Unwanted presents you feel guilty about throwing out*
- *Empty perfume bottles, half-empty jars of moisturiser*
- *Keys belonging to houses, flats and cars from years ago*
- *Rolled-up posters in the corner.*

Karen Kingston, author of *Clear Your Clutter With Feng Shui*, and *Creating Sacred Space With Feng Shui*, is an expert on this stuff. If you'd like to go the whole hog, and also clear the old vibes and stale energy from your bedroom, use her special rituals – which include clapping, ringing bells, lighting candles, burning incense, sprinkling holy water and offering flowers and prayers. For more information on this, see Karen's web site at www.spaceclearing.com.

The general idea of starting with a clean, uncluttered space is very important to feng shui. There is no point in sticking a crystal in your money corner if it's going to sit there with an old pet rock and a 1982 royals calendar. Be ruthless with every object in your room. Here's what to do:

1 *Look at it.*
2 *Does it bring your energy down or up?*
3 *If it brings you down, imagine the accumulated 'sagging'
   effect of seeing this thing ten times a day, 365 days a year.*

It may be the only photograph you have of the guy you spent two years of your life with, but if every time you see it you feel an energy drop, rip it up.

After the de-junking comes the boring bit. The vacu-uming, the mending and the window-washing. Then comes the slightly more interesting bit – visual cleaning.

Sit on the floor. Imagine a dazzling white light pouring in

through the light fitting on the ceiling, and filling the entire room. This is your universal cleaner. More powerful than Mr Sheen, it's superb for obliterating old vibes, bad vibes, and indifferent vibes. Make sure the light is as bright, white and pure as you can make it. Make sure you see it going under the bed and into the corners.

When you've finished, open the windows wide. You have just moved an awful lot of stuck, stale bedroom energy. A few people have told me that wonderful and strange things start happening just on the strength of this junk-chuck, clean-up and white-light exercise. Phones ring with job offers. Badly behaved boyfriends turn up with flowers. Party invitations land in the mailbox.

Now for the fun part. Look at the plan of your bedroom opposite.

What area of your life do you want to focus on? That's where you decorate, put flowers, light candles, burn incense or aromatherapy oil. That's where you hang a picture or photograph of something that makes you happy, or something which sums up what you'd like to see happening.

| money | fame | love |
|---|---|---|
| family | health | creativity |
| knowledge | career | friends |

◄ **The doorway is on this side of your room** ►

You can also do some problem-solving by avoiding the big feng shui no-nos:

1 *Don't have your feet pointing at the door from the bed.*
2 *Don't have a mirror facing you when you're in bed.*
3 *If there's a fan in the room, move your bed so you're not sleeping under the blades.*

People tie themselves into knots if their bedroom isn't a neat square or oblong. If you have a corner of the room missing (in an L-shaped bedroom, for example) don't panic. Just do what you can to dress up where that corner should be. If your money corner is missing, that's where you could put a beautiful vase on the floor, and fill it with the best flowers you can afford every week. If your love corner is missing, put a rose quartz crystal in there. Some people hang mirrors on the wall of the L-shaped bit to give the illusion that the space really does extend.

It's all about using your imagination, and your common sense. If you don't want to be single, don't put up a Picasso print of a single woman in your love corner!

I've known people to see results on the same day, and other people within a few weeks. I sorted out my office and moved stacks of my first novel, *Single White E-mail*, out of cardboard boxes and into my creativity corner. The book had dropped off the bestseller lists two months previously and I honestly thought that its time was over, which is probably why I'd stashed it away in boxes. Within three days of putting it in pride of place in my creativity corner, it zoomed back onto the bestseller list at number six.

Start small, with your bedroom. If good things begin to

happen for you, I recommend you go all the way and do your entire house and garden, or your flat. Karen Kingston and Lillian Too have both written great books on the subject.

## call a psychic cab

This works for me about nine times out of ten. You may find it happens ten times out of ten for you! The next time you are desperate for a cab, stand on the kerb and send this silent message out into the streets:

'I am (here) and I want to go (there). I have (x) dollars. I can wait for (x) minutes.'

This works if it's raining, if everybody is lining up on the road in front of you, and even if it's 3pm and there are no cabs on the road. Once, I didn't get a cab within my specified time (five minutes) but a friend 'happened' to drive past and gave me a lift instead. It helps if you visualise the cab pulling up in front of you, and you happily getting in.

## take an aura shower

This is good if you're feeling tired, stressed out, ill or otherwise fed up. If you do it properly you will feel the following within twenty minutes –

🔒 *Peace of mind*
🔒 *Mild bliss.*

I have watched people do this experiment, and some of them start smiling for no apparent reason. Other people have told me that they settle down and feel a bit more normal about life when they try it.

Lie down on the bed, or on the floor. Flop. Take three deep breaths. Flop again. Don't feel stupid or anxious about this. It's easy. Next, say these words in your head: 'What colour do I need?' The rule for this is – first thought, best thought! Don't agonise over it. Zoom in on the precise shade of that colour. If you chose blue, do you mean turquoise blue, or deep purple-blue?

Imagine that you have amazing rings on all your fingers, inlaid with jewels in that colour. See yourself wearing that colour. Take a bath in it. Feel it inside your body, as well as outside it. Stay with the colour for as long as you like. This is when some people start smiling involuntarily, while others find themselves letting out a long sigh, much to their surprise. This is a sign that the aura shower is working.

Ask again: 'What colour do I need?' If nothing comes up, you only needed one colour to correct your aura, and you can get up and carry on with your day. But you may get another colour, and another colour, and so on. Continue until you feel you're finished.

## wish books

Buy a notebook you really like. On a separate piece of scrap paper, write down a list of what you would like to happen in your life. Put in a lot of details. If you want to sketch something to show what you mean, then do that. Really think about what you're after. If you want a man who has a hairy chest and a wooden leg, write it down. Nobody else is going to see this, so what have you got to lose?

Using the scrap paper gives you a chance to be absolutely sure about what you want when you finally glue things, write things or draw things in your wish book. This is a special book, which will help to bring many (if not all) of your wishes about. So keep it clean, make sure it looks great, and hide it in a safe place.

Some people cut out photographs from magazines and stick them in their wish books. Others draw what they want. Feel free to add some of the details or notes you worked out on your scrap paper.

The rule with wish books is, if it's for the good of you

and the people around you, it will probably happen. What you're after is a win–win situation. Let's say you've cut out a picture of Nelson Mandela (for his integrity) and a picture of Brad Pitt (for his dimples), in your quest to dream up the ideal man. If a guy like this happens to be out there and also looking for someone like you, you'll meet.

If, on the other hand, your boyfriend has dumped you for no sensible reason, and you cut out a picture of a piranha fish and paste it over a photo of his groin, it's probably not going to happen. Win–win works. Win–groin mutilation tends to do nothing except create bad karma for you.

Here's a list of some of the things that have been wished into existence over the years – by people I know, and sometimes by me. Next to each real-life wish book example, I've written the time it took to come true.

- *A white beach house with blue and white tiles on the porch, and a rocking horse in the children's bedroom. (This was cut out of a magazine. It took eight months for the house and the rocking horse to arrive. The blue and white tiles didn't make it, though!)*
- *A pair of black leather pants like Jim Morrison's. (These were found on a market stall about a week later.*

*A classic win—win, as the guy who was selling the pants thought he'd never get rid of them.)*

🔒 *A fun romance in America. (This person got the fun, the romance and America almost two years after drawing a picture of it, complete with love hearts and the Statue of Liberty.)*

🔒 *A career with radio, TV, money, creativity and freedom. (I actually drew this for a friend and she e-mailed me two weeks later with this subject header — !!!!!!!!!! — to tell me it had happened.)*

🔒 *Two golden retriever puppies with pink ribbons round their necks. (OK, I admit it, I cut this out of a magazine and put it in my wish book. About three months later, I was walking past the local noticeboard and saw an advertisement asking for someone with spare time to walk a golden retriever. I did, and Max became one of my favourite canines in the whole world.)*

This last example shows something else about wish books — you might get part of the wish, rather than all of it, or it may come about in a surprising way.

## computer magic

If you have a screen-saver that allows you to make up a
sentence and put it on your computer, don't waste it. You
can use the same idea behind the wish book, and write
down something that you would like to see happen – then
watch it roll across your screen on a regular basis. I typed in
this sentence in bright pink: PARIS IN THE SPRING. I found
myself there last year, so it was definitely worth the effort.

People always ask me how this stuff works. I really don't
know, but when you consciously decide to take something
out of your head and write it down, draw it, or cut it out and
stick it in a book, the universe shifts. It works the other way
too. If you wander around with these ideas in your head –

- *I'm going to have to be lucky to pass my exam*
- *I'm hooked on cigarettes*
- *I always get the weirdos*

– well, does anything ever change?

The only rule with computer magic is your frame of
mind when you program your sentence into the machine.
If you feel pessimistic, uncertain, silly or embarrassed, it
won't work. The best attitude is either: total belief that it's

going to happen one day, though you have no idea how; or The Doris Day Approach – what will be, will be. In other words, it would be great if you got what you wanted, but you're not going to sink into despair if it doesn't happen.

The wish book win–win principle also applies to computers. If what you want is fine by other people as well as you, then it stands a better chance of happening. Giving up smoking is a good example – unless you're married to the head of Benson and Hedges, I guess.

## name your car

The chicks at Penguin Books swear by this and so do I. If you have trouble with mechanical or hi-tech objects – like cars, faxes, computers, laptops, microwave ovens, modems, plug-in aromatherapy burners and so on – name them. Mean what you say. Take your time to choose the name. Use it to communicate with your little mechanical or digital friend frequently. When I was having hassles with my laptop (the screen was wobbling and I was stuck in the country, far away from technical support), I gave it a name. Little Miranda. (The big computer is called Big Miranda.) I talked to Little Miranda and asked her to work for me. She stopped wobbling.

## reading pizzas

Do you want to see into the future? If tarot cards are a problem for you, and your dreams just aren't predictive, try pizza reading.

First, ask your question. Your psychic side will answer it for you, using symbols, images and ideas which you will see in the pizza. What you see in the cheese, the pepperoni and the mushrooms will be personal to you. If, for example, you see a door key, and that reminds you of your flatmate who is always forgetting his key, then that is a reference to him. Let your brain 'bounce' around images and ideas in a dreamy way. Make sure you write it all down, though. Time may well reveal that you have answered your own question about the future by what you saw on the day you did your pizza reading.

You can also read clouds. I did it on a long and boring flight from London to Moscow. The question I asked was, 'What will I find when I get to Moscow? What experiences will I have?' After a few minutes of staring at the clouds, I wrote down this:

- A man with a birthmark on his face
- Little kids with Hare Krishna ponytails
- Lots of dogs.

When we got to Moscow Airport, a man with a port wine birthmark on the left side of his face took our passports. I met the dogs the same night – a pack of hungry mongrels hanging around the hotel rubbish bins (they howled every night for a week, so they really were a major feature of my stay). The little kids with the Hare Krishna ponytails turned up on the second last day. They were in front of me at the queue for the ATM. Try cloud reading next time you fly – especially if they're not serving pizza.

## get back to me on this one

To finish the book, I'd like to try an experiment. Have you got a pen in your bag? Good. Look around the room, or the train, or the bus, or the plane (but hopefully not the car – this is a non-driving exercise).

Let your eyes settle on the first thing you see. It may be something quite boring, like a TV set, or quite detailed, like a piece of embroidery. Even a teacup will do.

Allow yourself to float off. What does this object or thing in front of you bring to mind? Without thinking too hard, write down your impressions in the space on the following page –

---

---

---

Don't edit yourself. If you're staring at a manila folder and it reminds you of your teacher at school with a beer gut, who reminds you of Foster's, which reminds you of foster homes, which reminds you of stray dogs, which reminds you of wanting to be a vet, then put it all down.

Now, turn this page upside down.

You have just answered the question, 'What happy choices are in store for me in the 21st century?'

If you are astounded (or if it comes true), I'd like to hear about it.

Please e-mail me at this address: jessica@zip.com.au.

And have a great millennium!